A TREATISE CONCERNING THE ARTE OF LIMNING

On previous page

WOODCUT BORDER of *The First and second volumes of Chronicles* by Raphael Holinshed (1574), probably designed by Hilliard (see monogram centre top). The border was used for several different titles in the sixteenth century. Original Size $11\frac{3}{5} \times 7\frac{3}{10}$ inches.

A TREATISE CONCERNING THE ARTE OF LIMNING

by NICHOLAS HILLIARD

together with

A MORE COMPENDIOUS DISCOURSE CONCERNING YE ART OF LIMING

by EDWARD NORGATE

with a parallel modernized text

edited by

R. K. R. THORNTON *and* T. G. S. CAIN

The Mid Northumberland Arts Group
Carcanet Press
1992

Mid Northumberland Arts Group ISBN 0 904790 76 2
Carcanet Press ISBN 0 85635 971 8

First published 1981 and in this edition 1992 by
The Mid Northumberland Arts Group, Wansbeck District Council,
Wansbeck Square, Ashington, Northumberland, NE63 9XL
and Carcanet Press Limited
208–212 Corn Exchange Buildings, Manchester, M4 3BQ

Printed by Short Run Press Ltd, Exeter.

CONTENTS

PREFACE

This book took its impetus from the Scottish Arts Council Exhibition of 1975 called 'A Kind of Gentle Painting'. There the work of Nicholas Hilliard and Isaac Oliver was set off against finely calligraphed phrases from Hilliard's *Treatise*, the manuscript of which was also exhibited, having made the short journey to Charlotte Square from the Edinburgh University Library. Those phrases whetted the appetite which no readily available publication could satisfy, and the discovery of the only published version showed that there was a need for an up-to-date critical edition. The publishers readily accepted the suggestion to publish the work and have been an unflagging help. Our debts since have been various: to the staff of Edinburgh University Library, in particular to Dr J.T.D. Hall, the Keeper of Special Collections; to the Department of Prints and Drawings at the British Museum, who saved us from making a conventional misattribution and helped us with the engravings; to the staffs of the British Library, the Bodleian, and the Victoria and Albert Museum, particularly to Mr V.J. Murrell, Mr John Murdoch, and Miss Anne Buddle; to Mr R.N. Orme; to the Duke of Buccleuch and the staff who were kind on our visit to the splendid collection at Bowhill; to the staff of Newcastle University Library; and to Dr Gillian Rogers of the Newcastle University Fine Art Department Library. We have incurred debts to earlier writers in the field, particularly to Erna Auerbach, Philip Pope-Hennessy, V.J. Murrell, Roy Strong, Graham Reynolds, and Martin Hardie. This second edition has been called for by a steady demand for the text. The economics of colour reproduction have meant that we have decided to leave out the illustrations in the interest of an affordable text, knowing that reproductions of Hilliard's work are readily available elsewhere.

ABBREVIATIONS

We have used the following abbreviations in our references to publications frequently cited in the text; here and throughout the book the place of publication is London unless otherwise stated:

Auerbach	Erna Auerbach, *Nicholas Hilliard* (1961)
Harley	R.D. Harley, *Artists' Pigments c.1600–1835* (1970)
Haydocke	Richard Haydocke, *A Tracte containing the Artes of curious Paintinge Caruinge & Buildinge* (Oxford, 1598). In references to Haydocke, however, we give the book reference, since the pagination begins again after the first book.
Miniatura	Edward Norgate, *Miniatura*, ed. Martin Hardie (1919)
Norman	Philip Norman (ed.), 'Nicholas Hilliard's Treatise Concerning "The Arte of Limning", with Introduction and Notes by Philip Norman, LL.D.', *Walpole Society*, I (1911–12), 1–54.
Pope-Hennessy	John Pope-Hennessy, 'Nicholas Hilliard and mannerist Art Theory', *JWCI*, VI (1943), 89–100
Thompson	D.V. Thompson, *The Materials of Medieval Painting* (1936)

INTRODUCTION

The Treatise

In the late sixteenth and early seventeenth centuries, many Englishmen considered the highest form of painting to be limning, the art of painting 'in small' in the traditional, largely opaque water colour medium described in our note on 'The Technique of Miniature Painting' below. It is surprising therefore that this *Treatise Concerning the Arte of Limning*, one of the most important and attractive documents in the history of English painting, written by Nicholas Hilliard, the outstanding English portrait painter of the reign of Elizabeth I, and without question one of the greatest English artists, should never have been published as a book in its own right. But that is the case; and it is published here in full and on its own for the first time.

We ought immediately to acknowledge the edition of the work and the scholarly introduction to it which Dr Philip Norman contributed to the *First Annual Volume of the Walpole Society* in 1912; but that volume is relatively inaccessible and Norman's text is a not altogether happy compromise. The following account of the manuscript and its author, some notes on where and in what forms the *Treatise* has appeared in print, and comments on the attribution of authorship of the two sections of the Edinburgh manuscript, will go some way to explain why it has not been given, and why it deserves, a place of its own.

The Edinburgh manuscript, the only known manuscript of Hilliard's work, contains two parts, of different dates and in different hands, and it is only the first part, the *Treatise* as we shall call it, which is Hilliard's; the second part, which we call the *More Compendious Discourse*, is a condensed version of a work by Edward Norgate, which we include to complete the transcription of the Edinburgh manuscript rather than to suggest that Hilliard had any part in it.

Hilliard's *Treatise* was probably written in response to a request for some account of the art of limning from Richard Haydocke, physician, Fellow of New College, and art lover.[1] In 1598 Haydocke published his translation of Giovanni Paolo Lomazzo's

Trattato dell'arte della pittura, scoltura ed architettura (Milan, 1584) under the title *A Tracte containing the Artes of curious Paintinge Caruinge & Buildinge* (Oxford, 1598). In his introduction 'To the Ingenuous Reader', Haydocke wishes for the '*skilfull pen of* George Vasarie', for

> *Then would M.* Nicholas Hilliards *hand, so much admired amongst strangers, striue for a comparison with the milde spirit of the late worldes-wonder* Raphaell Vrbine; *for* (*to speake a truth*) *his perfection in ingenuous* Illuminating *or* Limming, *the perfection of Painting, is* (*if I can iudge*) *so extraordinarie, that when I devised with my selfe the best argument to set it forth, I found none better, then to perswade him to doe it him selfe, to the viewe of all men by his pen; as hee had before vnto very many, by his learned pencell which in the ende hee assented vnto; and by mee promiseth you a treatise of his owne Practise that way, with all convenient speede.*

The *Treatise* has all the signs of being a gesture towards fulfilment of that promise. It opens with a reference to Lomazzo's work, and a promise that it will confine itself to limning; although it continues with a section on precious stones, this is not, it will be seen, at variance with that promise. The *Treatise* is not in Hilliard's hand, nor is it signed, but there is little doubt that the traditional attribution to Hilliard is correct. Internal evidence makes this clear: the mention of the personal interviews with Elizabeth I, whom Hilliard depicted many times; the continuation from limning to precious stones, specifically for gentlemen and goldsmiths (Hilliard was both goldsmith and limner); the praise of Holbein's style, whose 'manner of limning I have ever imitated, and hold it for the best' (p.49); the naming of Sir Christopher Hatton, whose portrait Hilliard limned; the reference to Sir John Harington's story of the drawing of Queen Elizabeth in four lines, which refers directly to Hilliard (see below, note 47). External evidence also points in the direction of Hilliard: several works on limning and painting quote recipes which are found in the *Treatise* and ascribe them to Hilliard; for example Norgate's *Miniatura* and many of the manuscripts associated with that work contain an appended recipe telling how 'To prepare Ceruse, Mr Hillyards way' which accords with the version on p.71 below. William Sanderson's *Graphice* (1658, pp.83–4) includes the note on pearl, on Black and the '*five perfect Colours, with their Lights and Shad-*

dowes' under the heading '*Excellent Receipts from Mr.* Hilliard, *that old famous English Limner.*' And Alexander Browne in *The Whole Art of Drawing* (1660, p.24) and in *Ars Pictoria* (1669, and in the edition of 1675 which with the exception of a few pages is reprinted from standing type or using old sheets, p.95) includes material on tempering colours and on the painting of pearls from the *Treatise* with the heading 'Additional Observations out of a *Manuscript* of Mr. *Hilliards* touching Miniture.' Internal and external evidence therefore combine with tradition in attributing the work to Hilliard. The relationship between the opinions expressed in the *Treatise* and what we know of his life and character, and the correspondence between the fastidious advice given and the neatness of his practice (Holbein is praised in the *Treatise* as being the 'neatest' master) strengthen the attribution beyond reasonable doubt.

The *Treatise* is not, however, the finished work that one might expect from Haydocke's promise. It savours of an unrevised version, like the early states of Norgate's work, combining more formal and rhetorical passages with personal observations, outbursts and what amount to grumblings on subjects where his feelings are roused or his professional pride is touched. There are three strands in the work as we have it: that of formal disquisition on the theory and status of limning, relating to Lomazzo and to the opening paragraphs of many works on art of the period; that of practical manual on methods and materials of painting, in which field it has interest because it is by Hilliard but must in content take second place to Norgate's work; and third, the element of personal complaint and self-revelation in which this *Treatise* is unique. The *Treatise* is also unusual in its linking of limning to the subject of precious stones, but there too the three elements of formal, technical and personal are in operation.

It is perhaps to this lack of finality that we owe the freshness of the *Treatise*. The information is addressed personally to the reader (perhaps Haydocke) as if responding to a list of enquiries: 'And now to the matter for precepts, for observations or directions to the art of limning, which you require as briefly and as plainly as I can' (p.53); and the *Treatise* may even include the questions: 'A word, I pray you, touching the making of those beautiful rubies or other stones, how you so artificially do them, that being never so little they seem precious stones, natural, clear and perspicuous; so that (by your favour) is no part of limning, wherefore require it not' (p.75). The two 'endings', that after the section on colours where 'I end with it' (p.81), and the 'Vale' after the section on precious stones after which come more questions and notes (one of the questions already answered), also suggest that Hilliard may have been writing in the form of replies to headings and questions proposed by someone like Haydocke. Ends not tied up and inconsistencies strengthen the impression that this is an early draft: we are not given the argument on the relative worthiness of painting and carving which we are promised 'in the last leaf' (p.51), and colours which are called, 'naught for limning' in the introductory note on colours – verditer, pink, sap-green and litmus – are nonetheless included later (see note 52).

The *Treatise* makes some gestures towards the rhetorical and formal aspects with which one is familiar from other works of the period: the justification of limning by reference to Exodus and to the Classics, in particular to the career of Quintus Fabius Pictor; the discussion of the relative merits of painter and sculptor; even the complaint of the small reward and too low status of the limner is conventional. But it is its combination of elegance, information, personal forthrightness and spirited observation which most attracts our attention to the *Treatise* and demands, as both art history and jewel among treatises, a setting of its own.

Nicholas Hilliard

Despite his prominence, relatively little is known about Hilliard's life, although various modern scholars, especially Erna Auerbach, have added a good deal to the very meagre information available until recently. He was born in Exeter in 1546 or 1547; both his father, Richard, and grandfather, John Wall, were prosperous goldsmiths, and Nicholas himself was to become a practising goldsmith, as were two of his brothers, John and Jeremy. Most of his formative years were spent in the household of a goldsmith, first that of his father, and then from the age of fifteen, that of Robert Brandon, to whom he was apprenticed from 1562 to 1569. He continued to refer to himself as goldsmith as well as painter for the rest of his life, and the background of the goldsmith's shop is, as will be seen, of crucial importance to an understanding of Hilliard's art.

His father, Richard, was a considerable figure in the Exeter community; in a flourishing city which had a large number of goldsmiths he built up a practice which was second only to that of the prolific John Jones. In 1556 he became a bailiff of the city, and in 1568 its sheriff. He appears to have been a strong Protestant, and as such was involved in the siege of Exeter during the Catholic rising of 1549 against the Protestant Prayer Book of Edward VI. Also involved in this fighting was a still more prominent member of the Exeter merchant community, John Bodley, father of the Thomas Bodley who founded the Bodleian Library. John Bodley was a thoroughgoing Calvinist, who was later forced to leave England at some time between 1553 and 1555, to escape persecution during the reign of Mary. According to Sir Thomas Bodley's account his father subsequently called over 'my Mother, with all his children and Family, whom he settled for a time at Wesel in Cleveland'[2] in north-west Germany. As part of this 'family' on an early and fortuitous version of the Grand Tour went, it would seem, the young Nicholas Hilliard. The group moved on to Frankfurt, and finally to Geneva, where their arrival is recorded in the *Livre des Anglois à Genève*: '8th of May, 1557: John Bodleigh . . . his wife, Thomas, John and Lawrence his Sonnes, Prothese his daughter, John Boggens and Richard Vivian his servants, and Elenor his maide. Nicholas, brother to the said John Bodleghe. Nicholas Hilliarde. Augustine Brodebreche. Percival Wiburn.' (ed. J. Southerden Burn, 1831, p.10).

It is not known at what date Bodley's family joined him in exile, but it is likely to have been 1555 or 1556. The family did not return to England until after the accession of Elizabeth in 1558, John Bodley receiving permission to leave Geneva on 5th September, 1559.[3] Assuming that Hilliard remained with the family, he would have spent a minimum of three years abroad – between the ages of nine and twelve. Holbein had left Switzerland thirty years earlier because of its iconoclastic atmosphere, and Calvin's Geneva was hardly the best place for an aspiring painter to visit. Nevertheless the journey can only have widened Hilliard's knowledge of art, Dutch and German art in particular. He probably also shared to some degree the thorough education which the Bodley children received in Geneva; the initial attempt at a rhetorical ordering of the *Treatise* and its classical references, though commonplace enough, would support the idea of an education in a gentleman's family, as would Hilliard's strong claim to gentlemanly status for the limner. In Geneva he would have found himself among a distinguished and very active group of exiles, led by John Knox, and including Sir Francis Knollys, first cousin by marriage of the future Queen Elizabeth, and other members of the Knollys family, which was later to be prominent in Elizabeth's court. The most lasting monument of the work of this exiled group was the famous Geneva Bible, sometimes called the Bodley Bible, in the printing and licensing of which in 1560 John Bodley was a leading figure.

Hilliard's connection with the Bodley family may not have ended in 1559; indeed if, as seems probable, he had been taken into the household as a page there is no reason why it should have done. Bodley settled in London on his return, and it may well have been there, rather than in Exeter, that Nicholas painted in 1560 the three earliest of his miniatures that survive, two self-portraits 'aetatis suis 13', and a copied portrait of the executed Edward Seymour, Duke of Somerset, who as Protector had been responsible for the imposition of the Prayer Book of which Bodley had been so ardent a supporter and which had caused the 1549 rebellion. Not only does the choice of subject seem appropriate to Bodley's Calvinist circle, but the miniature is clearly a copy of a Holbein or Holbeinesque original, something much more likely to have been available in London than in Exeter. As we have seen, Hilliard speaks in the *Treatise* of his imitation of 'Holbein's manner of limning', and there must be a strong presumption that during these years he had a privileged access to other Holbein miniatures, an access that might have been gained with Bodley's help, if not that of some still more influential figure, such as Sir Francis Knollys, who may later have stood as godfather to one of Hilliard's children.[4]

In the *Treatise* Hilliard writes of the way in which a perceptive father can encourage an aptitude for limning from an early age (p.45). Such perceptiveness on his own father's part may well have been what led to the next important step in his career, his apprenticeship in 1562 to Robert Brandon, the Queen's jeweller and one of the leading English goldsmiths of his time. The fact that Brandon was a jeweller is of great importance, for it is in this field that the arts of the goldsmith and the miniature painter come into closest contact. Indeed, for the Elizabethans the miniature was a kind of jewel, and was frequently treated and spoken of as such: 'Here, wear this jewel for me, 'tis my picture' says Olivia in *Twelfth Night* (III.iv.228), pointing also to one of the most important functions of the miniature as an intimate token of affection. Hilliard himself speaks of the miniature as 'fittest . . . to put in jewels of gold' (p.43), in just the same way as precious stones or enamels were set by the goldsmith, and the Drake Pendant or the ornate Armada Jewel are good examples of his work being placed in very rich settings which are themselves assumed to have been made by him.[5] In *Aspects of Miniature Painting* (Copenhagen, 1953), T.H. Colding argued persuasively that we should see the art of the miniaturist as closely related to the art of the goldsmith, with the painted 'jewel' of the miniature developing from the translucent enamels on an engraved ground, and the *verres eglomisés* (glass over gold leaf on which a picture was engraved and coloured) used by earlier and contemporary goldsmiths.[6]

Hilliard's career, his work, and what he writes here in the *Treatise*, all serve to strengthen the broad outlines of Colding's argument. The shape and setting of his miniatures, their range of colours and tones, the preference of line over 'hard shadows' (p.67), the attempt to give 'the true lustre to pearl and precious stone' so that 'it seemeth to be the thing itself' (p.43), all point to the close link between Hilliard's art and that of the goldsmith. So too does the long section of the *Treatise* which he devotes to precious stones, a section specifically concerned with the relationship of those stones to the colours which he uses in the miniatures, colours which can be seen as surrogates for the stones themselves in the same way that enamels were. Later, writing to Robert Cecil, Hilliard clearly sees himself as a goldsmith-painter guarding the secrets of his trade, as opposed to the more conventional painters, who would not be competent, he says, to trim Elizabeth's tomb:

> 'I requested to haue the trymyng of the sayde Toumbe, because as a Goldsmith I understand howe to set foorthe & garnishe a peece of stone woork not with muche gylding to hyde the beawty of the stone, but where it may grace the same, and no more. And having scill to make more radient cullors like vnto Ammells [enamels], then yet is to Paynters knowne, I would have taught sum one which woulde not

have made it common' (Salisbury MS.119.8, 1606).

Though it has been felt that to see the miniature painter as related to the jeweller in this way is somehow to detract from Hilliard's status as a great painter,[7] this was not the way he or his contemporaries saw the matter. In England in particular limning was regarded by many as the highest form of visual art. Painters who worked on a larger scale were still associated to some extent with interior decorators; the office of Serjeant Painter to the Crown involved a great deal of decorative painting, gilding coaches, painting coats of arms, and so forth.[8] Hilliard, though he too was in all probability involved in such work, is at pains in the *Treatise* to dissociate limning from this kind of painting, seeing it as a higher and a more gentlemanly activity: 'It is sweet and cleanly to use, and it is a thing apart from all other painting or drawing, and tendeth not to common men's use, either for furnishing of houses, or any patterns for tapestries, or building, or any other work whatsoever. And yet it excelleth all other painting whatsoever in sundry points' (p.43). The relatively low social status of the painter in Elizabethan England, and the concomitantly low financial rewards, go a long way to explain the mediocre quality of much native work, and make it no surprise that the greatest English-born painter of the period should be a miniaturist who saw himself as belonging to a quite distinct tradition from the painters 'in large'. Thus when Hilliard speaks of Holbein,[9] it is as both a 'painter and limner,' the 'greatest master truly in both those arts after the life that ever was' (p.49). It is with this distinction in mind that one should read the opening lines of the *Treatise*: Lomazzo has covered one kind of art, painting; Hilliard will cover limning, not a minor branch of painting, but a distinct form of at least equal status to conventional painting. In the work of his pupil Isaac Oliver the distinction is less clear cut; Oliver's greater degree of shadowing, less gem-like finish, and softer modelling of features all link his work with painting 'in large', and differentiate it from that of Hilliard, in whose work one is always more conscious that the miniature is designed 'to be viewed in hand' (p.67).

Equally distinctive in Hilliard's work is the consciousness of pattern playing against the realism, the ovals of the frames echoing in the circles and ellipses of the ruffs, collars, faces, lettering and hats (even the unusual rectangle of the 'Unknown Man, aged

24 in 1572' in the V&A, is used along with the lettering to emphasize the haughty verticals of the neck and cheek and the horizontal of the hat). Only in the 'Unknown Lady' (Fitzwilliam), in 'George Clifford, 3rd Earl of Cumberland' (National Maritime Museum) and above all in the 'Unknown Youth, "Young man among roses" ' (V&A) does Hilliard successfully translate into a slightly larger scale this intimate relationship of the picture with its setting.

It should not come as a surprise, therefore, to find Hilliard being apprenticed to a goldsmith rather than a member of the guild of Painter-Stainers: as Mary Edmond has shown recently, it was not uncommon even for those who were to become best known as painters 'in large' to be apprenticed to goldsmiths.[10] Brandon's workshop must have been more sophisticated than that of Richard Hilliard, and may well have been chosen because it was here that Nicholas's evident talents as a limner could best be encouraged. The suggestion (Auerbach, p.5) that he first learnt his craft from an illuminator of manuscripts before going to Brandon is not a necessary hypothesis, though it does make a suggestive link with the earlier English tradition of manuscript illumination. Hilliard in fact probably did receive instruction from a limner outside of Brandon's shop, someone like Levina Teerlinc, or even earlier from his fellow Devonian John Shute: limners who were not also goldsmiths would in any case have had to collaborate with such a man as Brandon over the important question of the setting of their work. But it is quite possible that just as Hilliard taught his own son Laurence, Rowland Lockey, Oliver, John Bettes the younger, and doubtless others, to paint while they were apprenticed to him as a Freeman of the Goldsmiths' Company, so he was taught in part by Brandon or someone else in his workshop. Certainly it would be a mistake to see his apprenticeship as a digression from his career as a limner. At the very least he would have had to design and make preparatory drawings (including portraits, presumably) for engravings, jewels, medals and seals.

In Hilliard's case at least designs drawn or 'invented' by him were sometimes engraved by another craftsman: thus two of the engraved title pages collected by R.B. McKerrow and F.S. Ferguson in *Title-Page Borders Used in England and Scotland, 1485–1640* (1932) would appear to have been drawn by him and cut by someone with the initials 'C.T.'. One, dated 1574, has a prominent 'NH' monogram (see half-title page above: McKerrow and Ferguson, facs. 148): the other, for a book dated 1571, has only C.T.'s initials, but is so close in conception and quality that it seems likely to have been designed by the same hand (McKerrow and Ferguson, facs. 133).[11] Evidence of Hilliard's contact with a prominent engraver, John Rutlinger or Rutlingen, comes in the same year, 1571, in the minutes of the Goldsmiths' Company, when John's wife promises to deliver 'vnto Thomas Clerke a booke of portraitures wthin this sennyght wholle and perfett, which is now in the handes of Nichas Helliard' (quoted in Auerbach, p.6). The nature of this book is not clear, but it is obviously tempting to see Hilliard in the role of drawer or 'inventor' of portraits which Rutlinger was to engrave.

Rutlinger was, like Hilliard, a goldsmith, and the engraving techniques which Hilliard would have learnt as a goldsmith are a major influence on his art: his liking for a clear, precise line, and his method of shadowing by hatching (see *Treatise* pp.65 and 81) both stem from this training. Hence his at first sight slightly surprising insistence that the apprentice limner should learn by copying Dürer's engravings so closely that 'one shall not know the one from the other, that he may be able to handle the pencil point [i.e. the paintbrush] in like sort' (p.81). It is significant, in this context, that most of the artists to whom Hilliard refers in the *Treatise* were at this time better known as engravers than as painters. At least two of them, Albrecht Dürer, and Lambert Suavius, were also the sons of master goldsmiths, while another, Holbein, made numerous designs for jewellery and plate (Botticelli, Verocchio and Ghirlandaio were among the many other Renaissance artists who began their careers as goldsmiths).

When Hilliard became a Freeman of the Goldsmiths' Company in 1569 he began working on his own account as both goldsmith and limner. In 1570 he took his first apprentice, and seems at this time to have been working with his brother John, who had also served his time with a London goldsmith. It is possible that Nicholas began working for the Queen even before his apprenticeship ended; his first dated portrait of her (Nat. Portrait Gall.) was done in 1572, a portrait that is almost certainly from the life, and thus may well be the product of that sitting 'in the open alley of a goodly garden' which is described in the

Treatise (p.67), and which was, if we are to believe him, to have such a profound effect on his views on the matter of shadowing. Whether he adopted the Queen's aesthetic views or vice versa, it is certain that from this time until the end of his life Hilliard was firmly established in the royal service, the dominant figure in English painting. He was, indeed, unique amongst English painters in being consistently recognised by his contemporaries as at least the equal of any of the foreign artists who, by their presence or reputation, were otherwise to dominate English painting until the coming of Hogarth. Neither Oliver nor Cooper was quite to equal his eminence: Donne's comment in *The Storme* that 'a hand, or eye / By *Hilliard* drawne, is worth an history, / By a worse painter made' (ll.3–5) is only the most famous of many references to Hilliard by contemporary writers. Henry Constable compares him to Michaelangelo and Raphael in a sonnet whose praise might be taken as merely hyperbolic were it not echoed by the more considered enthusiasm of Richard Haydocke, who in the passage already quoted also makes the comparison with Raphael, and sees Hilliard as the perfect master of what Haydocke considers to be 'the perfection of Painting.' Sir John Harington, like Haydocke, takes limning 'to be the verie perfection' of the art of painting, and sees Hilliard as not only comparable with any living painter, but one up on Apelles in his ability to draw Elizabeth's likeness from memory (see below, note 47).

Haydocke's reference to Hilliard's reputation abroad ('amongst strangers') is borne out in France by the words of the scholar, translator and alchemist Blaise de Vigenère, who describes him as 'tenu pour l'un des plus excellents dont on aye mémoire au moins en petit volume' (Auerbach, p.15). In Spain the art theorist and teacher of Velasquez, Francisco Pacheco, is almost certainly describing a Hilliard miniature when he writes, with the rubric 'Singular iluminacion:'

> 'this city enjoys possession of a small portrait, taken from the life, of an English boy, which today belongs to the Prebendary Diego Vidal; framed in ivory, it is oval on a blue ground, with some letters of powdered gold; the head is done with such skill, power, and smoothness [*destreza, fuerza y suavidad*] that in my opinion it leaves far behind it whatever has been seen in this genre. I say truly that it seems to me that limning can advance no further, and that the art ended

> there. The Master who did it was an Englishman, but there is no note of his name, which for this alone should be ever-living.'[12]

It is, as Roy Strong stays (*Nicholas Hilliard*, p.1975, p.19), the most moving of all the tributes paid to Hilliard by his contemporaries.

If there is never any suggestion of Hilliard having to struggle for recognition, he seems to have struggled financially throughout his life, partly due to the notorious parsimony of his royal patron, partly due to his own apparent readiness to stand as surety for the debts of others, and partly no doubt due to the discrepancy, feelingly described in an obviously autobiographical passage in the *Treatise* (pp.87–9), between the work and life-style of a great painter and the actual rewards. Three to four pounds was the normal rate for a Hilliard miniature, without an elaborate setting, while the Queen's patronage meant so little financially that Hilliard was to tell Cecil in 1601 that 'if the common work for other persons had not been more profitable' he could not have afforded the privilege of being the Queen's limner (Salisbury MS. 87.25). Royal promises of reversions of offices, tithes, leases and so forth came frequently enough, but seem largely to have been ways of avoiding any more tangible form of payment. Many artists who worked for the crown under both Elizabeth and James did so at a loss, particularly in the expensive field of jewellery and goldsmith's work. The accounts of Sir William Herrick (Bodleian MS. Eng. Hist. b.216. c.474–484), one of Brandon's successors as jeweller to the crown, and uncle of the poet (who was also an apprentice goldsmith), show huge sums owed to him by James I. Some of these may arise from the goldsmith's second profession of banker and moneylender, but it seems probable that it was mainly the prestige involved that made it worthwhile for any artist to serve the crown under Elizabeth or James. The passage in the *Treatise* defending artists against the charge of being 'unthrifts' (p.89), and contrasting the lack of support received in England with that found on the Continent, is an understandable expression of frustration at the system which could lead a great and acknowledged painter like Hilliard to pawn one of his own miniatures (a portrait, ironically, of James I) to this same Sir William Herrick for forty shillings (Bodl. MS. Eng. Hist. b.216. c.477, fols. 75–6), or at the age of fifty-four to seek permission to live abroad for a year or two to avoid his creditors.

This, however, is to anticipate; though creditors never seem to have been far behind Hilliard even at the outset of his career, it was not to escape them that he made his second recorded trip abroad in 1576. In July of that year he married Alice Brandon, imitating his father and many other favoured apprentices in marrying a daughter of his former master, and in the autumn of that year he travelled to France with his wife. It was presumably there that he painted the superb self-portrait of 1577 (V&A) and the fine miniatures of his father and his new wife Alice (V&A). He went to France with the Queen's blessing, and in 1577 was in the service of Elizabeth's suitor, Francois, Duke of Alençon and Anjou, in whose household accounts he figures as 'Nicholas Béliart, peintre anglois.' Later, probably between 1581 and 1583, he was to paint the portraits of the Duke and Elizabeth at each end of a now lost Prayer Book in which the Queen herself had written prayers in different languages (a black and white facsimile of 1893 is in the British Library). During his two years in France, much of which was spent in Paris, Hilliard was in close touch with French artists. He appears to have stayed with the great goldsmith and medallist Germain Pilon, to have met Jacques Gaultier, the painter, and through him the engraver Léonard Gaultier. He refers in the *Treatise* to a meeting with Ronsard (p.49), while one of his greatest admirers, Blaise de Vigenère, negotiated with him to provide engraved portraits of the Duke and Duchess of Nevers.

The question of French influence on Hilliard's work is a vexed one. Pilon's medals certainly appear, as Carl Winter has suggested, to have influenced the portrait of Richard Hilliard and the self-portrait, in which echoes of Dürer's self-portraits of 1493 and, especially, 1498 are also evident. It is often argued that François Clouet, too, exerted a strong influence even before Hilliard's visit to France: but while Hilliard doubtless did learn something from the freedom and informality of Clouet's drawings, his debt to the French painter has perhaps been overstated. It is interesting to note that no French artist is mentioned in the *Treatise*, though Hilliard is generous enough in his acknowledgement of those from whom he has learnt, or whose work he admires. One of the latter is Giambattista Rossi, leading figure in the school of Fontainebleau; and the suggestion that Hilliard's best-known miniature, the 'Young Man Among Roses' (V&A)

was influenced by another Fontainebleau artist, Primaticcio, is lent some weight by Hilliard's praise of Rossi, with its implication that he had visited Fontainebleau.[13]

It seems likely that French influences have been emphasized at the expense not only of Hilliard's acknowledged masters, Dürer and Holbein, but also of Flemish painters such as Antonio Mor and Steven van der Meulen, both of whom were much admired in English court circles during the period of Hilliard's apprenticeship. Graham Reynolds has rightly drawn attention to the striking relationship between Mor's fine portrait of Sir Henry Lee, done in 1568 (National Portrait Gallery) and Hilliard's equally accomplished 'Unknown Man aged 24 in 1572' (V&A; see Reynolds, *English Portrait Miniatures*, 1952, p.18). Though Hilliard must have disliked the heavy shadowing of much of van der Meulen's work, he seems to have taken from him in particular the characteristic pose which gives a sharp, dramatic angle to the sitter's face, with the eyes turned as if in a sudden glance, sometimes haughty, sometimes intimate, towards the spectator. The portraits of Leicester, a patron of both artists, by van der Meulen and Hilliard are particularly close in this respect (see Roy Strong, *Tudor and Jacobean Portraits*, 1969, plates 378, 379 and 386). Even closer to Hilliard's 1576 miniature of Leicester (National Portrait Gallery) is the portrait painted at about the same date by an unknown painter, very much in the same Flemish tradition, in the National Portrait Gallery.

At about the end of his stay in France Hilliard's first child Daniel was born; between 1578 and 1588 he and Alice were to have seven children, of whom only one, Laurence, followed him as a goldsmith and miniaturist. Laurence was a family name; the names of the other children may reflect Hilliard's standing at court, with Elizabeth, Francis, Lettice, Penelope and Robert all suggesting courtly and possibly even royal godparents. Elizabeth herself, Cecil, Leicester, Walsingham, and Essex – all the most powerful figures in the court – patronised him at various times during Elizabeth's reign, not merely by sitting to him, but by intervening on his behalf in a variety of ways. Other influential courtiers like Sidney and Hatton are mentioned in the *Treatise*, while there are fine surviving miniatures of Sir Walter Raleigh, Francis Drake, Sir Anthony Mildmay, the Earls of Cumberland, Southampton, Devonshire and (probably) Northumberland, and many others who were close in their various ways to the centre of power. If we allow for the numerous miniatures which are known to have been lost, and others of which no record exists, then it seems likely that few courtiers of any consequence did not have their portrait painted by Hilliard between 1570 and 1600. In the years following the Queen's death the situation seems to have been slightly different, with Hilliard's pupil Isaac Oliver becoming more fashionable among the *cognoscenti* of the Jacobean court. But during Elizabeth's reign at least, Hilliard held the centre of the stage in a way which few other English painters have ever done.

His position was such that it does not now seem surprising that he should have been given the highly prestigious task of designing the second Great Seal of Elizabeth in 1584, a commission more important in Elizabethan eyes than the painting of portraits. At the time, however, it was resented: in the letter to Cecil about the trimming of Elizabeth's tomb he refers to the envy which this commission caused 'for my doing well in other men's offices'. Perhaps more important, the work on the seal was apparently expensive and took him into yet more financial difficulties. He had already lost money by what now seems the slightly ludicrous method of investing in Scottish gold mines, and now bonds became forfeit, and money had to be borrowed from Brandon, by this time Chamberlain of the City.

Brandon died only a few years later, in 1591, and Hilliard's state of apparently chronic insolvency is no doubt the reason for his surprising and total exclusion from his father-in-law's will. Though a fairly rich man, Brandon went to great lengths to ensure that the fifty pounds he left Alice should be paid to her in instalments by the Goldsmiths' Company, and should not go to Hilliard or even to his children. It may be that, as is generally assumed, there was something of the antipathy of careful businessman to careless artist in Brandon's relationship with Hilliard. But Brandon was himself an artist, and a more practical explanation of his will may be that it was designed to prevent Hilliard's creditors from getting the money that Brandon wished to leave not to them, but to his daughter. The fact that Nicholas's grandson, also a goldsmith, and born after Richard Brandon's death, was named Brandon Hilliard suggests that there was no deep or lasting animosity.

Hilliard's own father was not driven to such lengths, making Nicholas his principal male heir when he died in 1594, leaving him all his property in Exeter, together with the patronage of the tiny church of St Pancras (surviving incongruously today in the middle of a modern shopping centre). Being a patron may have bolstered those pretensions to gentility which Hilliard is so keen to emphasize in the *Treatise*, but otherwise the bequest does not seem to have solved his financial problems. Between 1595 and 1600 he was at loggerheads with the Goldsmiths' Company over the renewal of the lease of his house, 'The Maydenhead', in Gutter Lane where he lived and worked from 1578 till 1613, when Laurence took over the house and shop, and Nicholas moved to the parish of St Martin-in-the-Fields. He had been driven to mortgage the existing lease of the house in about 1590; eventually this mortgage was redeemed for him by the Earl of Essex, but the Goldsmiths' Company was markedly unwilling to renew the lease. Only pressure of the very highest kind, from Elizabeth via the Privy Council, eventually secured it in 1600, and then only on condition that Hilliard should paint for the Company 'a faire picture in greate of her Matie to remayne in the Howse for an ornam't and remembrance as well of their humble duties as of her princelie fauor towardes him and of his gratefulnes to the Company' (Auerbach, p.29). This condition, together with the passage in the *Treatise* in which Hilliard speaks of his own technique for painting pearls in oils (p.71), provide the only firm evidence that Hilliard painted on a large scale as well as in miniature. Nothing further is heard of this picture, nor could Hilliard meet the other condition of renewal – the payment of thirty pounds – until 1602.

In 1601 Hilliard was unsuccessfully seeking the Queen's permission to go abroad again to escape his creditors, despite the fact that an annuity of forty pounds a year had finally been granted to him by the Crown through the mediation of Cecil, who appears to have been his most constant patron at this time. Even this annuity was paid direct to other men, presumably creditors, for some years. According to the very revealing letter to Cecil in which the request for permission to go abroad is made, Hilliard's affairs were altogether at a low ebb, with even his long acknowledged supremacy as a miniaturist being threatened by his own pupils. After pointing out how costly it has been for him to work in the royal service, he goes on to say that 'hoping to bring up others for Her Majesty's better service, I have taught divers, both strangers and English, which now and of a long time have pleased the common sort exceeding well, so that I am myself become unable by my art any longer to keep house in London without some further help of Her Majesty' (Salisbury MS. 87.25). Appeals to Elizabeth's purse had, of course, to be worded in extravagant terms, and it may be that Hilliard exaggerates the degree to which he is being eclipsed by, presumably, Isaac Oliver. But the *Treatise*, written at about the same date as this letter, also glances feelingly at the 'botchers' who devalue the work of the skilled craftsman so that 'good workmen give over to use their best skill, for all men carry one price' (p.43).

Although Oliver could hardly be described as a botcher, there are times when one feels that Hilliard has 'given over to use his best skill' in miniatures painted after about 1600. There is certainly no uniform decline: miniatures such as those of Lady Elizabeth Stanley and Charles I as Prince of Wales, the latter painted in 1614, show that it was not advancing age that made some other portraits of James I and his court seem rather pedestrian when compared to Hilliard's best work. Even if Oliver was in the ascendancy, however, Hilliard remained James I's limner and medallist (the latter activity taking up more of his time than hitherto) until the end of his life. And if he was conscious of becoming unfashionable as well as poorer, there is no strong evidence that his reputation diminished significantly either during these years up to his death, or even during the rest of the century. As late as 1688 John Aubrey was to give the Ashmolean a portrait of 'Archbishop Bancroft's, by Hillyard, the famous illuminer in Queen Elizabeth's time'.[14] On the whole Hilliard's greatness as a miniature painter has rarely been in question from the time when he first emerged as a mature painter in the 1570s. As always in his career, however, reputation did not bring commensurate prosperity during the last years of his life: in 1617 he finally suffered the indignity of imprisonment in Ludgate for debt. In his will, made on Christmas Eve 1618, he left money (or, to be exact, money owed to him) to his sister, Anne Avery, a pound to the poor of St Martin-in-the-Fields, and household goods to the value of ten pounds to his servant, Elizabeth Deacon, who had nursed him in his last illness. The rest of the estate went to Laurence, making it almost certain that Alice Hilliard had died before this date. Indeed, it is probable that Nicholas had married again, and that his second wife had also predeceased him. The elaborate inscription on his portrait of Alice refers to her as his first wife, while an entry in the Parish Register of St Mary at Hill, London, quoted a little mistrustingly by Auerbach (p.40), records a marriage between a Nicholas Hilliard and Susan Gysard in 1608. Gysard was the family name of three goldsmiths working in London at this time; this fact, combined with the inscription on Alice's portrait, would seem to confirm that he did indeed remarry.[15] The will, however, suggests that Susan Hilliard was dead by 1618. A few days after it was made, Nicholas Hilliard himself died at the age of seventy-two or seventy-three; he was buried at St Martin-in-the-Fields on 7th January, 1618/19.

The Manuscript and its History

The manuscript of Hilliard's *Treatise*, in the Edinburgh University Library, number Laing III 174, consists of 16 pages measuring 12⅝ inches by 8 inches, on paper with a Strasbourg watermark corresponding to type 7210 in C.M. Briquet's *Les Filigranes* (facsimile of 1907 edition, Amsterdam, 1968, vol. I, p.395). The *Treatise* is written in a hand which is consistent with the date of 1624 which is appended to it, by a scribe who shows little evidence of much intelligence or great care; several emendations must be made to make sense of parts of it, and can be made by reference to other works, other versions of parts of the *Treatise*, correct versions of proper names or simply to the context. The title of the first part is not contemporary with the body of the text but is in the hand of George Vertue, the eighteenth-century engraver and antiquary who once owned the manuscript; it is possible that he copied it from a lost outside page, since he has also, with some appearance of authority, copied the missing pieces into the torn first page (see pp.41 and 42).

The *Treatise* must have been written soon after Haydocke's promise of it in 1598, and at any rate before the death of Queen Elizabeth on 24th March 1602/3. The nomenclature of the colours is consistent with this date, in that Hilliard uses 'ceder green' and 'Indy blew', names which became obsolete in the early seventeenth century, and the use of burnt fruit stone blacks is said to argue for a date very near to the sixteenth century (see

Harley, pp.3–4 but note Norgate's continued use of them). This places it at a stage in Hilliard's career when he was more than usually troubled by financial difficulties, and by the threat to his pre-eminence posed by his own pupil, Isaac Oliver.

All traces of this manuscript are lost until it came into the possession of George Vertue in the eighteenth century; but evidence of wider circulation of Hilliard's work is available in both printed and manuscript sources. In 1634 John Bate wrote a fascinating book of water works, fire works and mechanical and artistic wonders half way between medieval witchcraft and Victorian parlour magic, called *The Mysteries of Nature and Art*; the second edition of 1635 added to its 'Third Booke of Drawing, Limming, Colouring, Painting, and Graving' two long sections which derive from a version of the Hilliard *Treatise*. Bate does not acknowledge the author (merely noting on the title page of the third book that he has added instructions from 'other collections that I have gathered from time to time out of such as have written on this subject' [p.139]), nor does he always understand him, as for example on the subject of 'Empresse work', nor do the passages provide us with convincing variant readings although they seem to derive from a different manuscript; but Bate does re-order and summarise the material and add two short passages which seem unlikely to be Hilliard's, according as they do with Bate's mechanical taste and suggesting an uncharacteristic sootiness of shadow.[16] William Sanderson in *Graphice. The use of the Pen and Pensil* (1658) uses material on the painting of pearl and on the five perfect colours. Alexander Browne quotes a small part in *Ars Pictoria* (1669 and 1675), William Salmon repeats the passage on pearl in his *Polygraphice* (1672), and a version of other passages appears in a book of 1664. This last version, abbreviated and summarised as Norgate's was for the *More Compendious Discourse*, is printed in *A Drawing Book: or, The Pencil Improved*, whose unnamed author states on the title page that

> In the Limning Part, you have from a Manuscript which came happily to hand out of the Collection of Mr. *Garrat*, Limner to Queen *Elizabeth*, the Perfect Discourse how to prepare, mix, and work all those Colours, with Directions what Lights to use in Drawing by the Life, with the Height and Distance the Party ought to stand you intend to Draw.

Mr Garrat is obviously Marcus Gheeraerts the Younger (fl.1561–

1635), and the copy used, although much abbreviated, is in a few of its readings nearer to the original than the Edinburgh manuscript.

Although Vertue had made a vast collection of material, and his notes both on and about that material show the amount of work he had done on it, he had not carried out his design of writing a history of painting when he died in 1757. The collection was bought from Vertue's widow by Walpole, and remained at Strawberry Hill until the dispersal sale of 1842. The manuscript then passed into the hands of Patrick Fraser Tytler, and then into the hands of David Laing, who bequeathed it to Edinburgh University Library, to whom it was delivered in 1879.

Walpole made a little use of the manuscript in his *Anecdotes of Painting*, and some more if slightly inaccurate use was made of this and the manuscripts associated with Norgate's work by the Rev. James Dallaway in an edition of the *Anecdotes* in 1826–8; but it was not until the present century that Dr Phillip Norman gave full publicity to the manuscript, culminating in his editing a version of the whole manuscript for the Walpole Society, published in their *Transactions* in 1912. Norman's sensible and for the most part convincing 'Introductory Note' precedes a text which is reasonably reliable in its readings but departs from its original mainly in the question of capital letters, punctuation – which in the original is both scant and erratic – and paragraphing, though we ought to point out that he ignored completely the scribe's deliberate attempts at italic for certain key words. Norman's remains a useful edition and is the only attempt at a full one, but various writers have edited sections for themselves, most notably Erna Auerbach in her *Nicholas Hilliard* (1961) and Roy Strong in *Nicholas Hilliard* (1975).

The More Compendious Discourse

The *More Compendious Discourse*, the second part of the Edinburgh manuscript, is not by Hilliard (though scholars like Dr Philip Norman and Erna Auerbach have suggested it was), but by Edward Norgate (?1580/1–1650), the author of *Miniatura*, the revised text of which was written between December 1648 and October 1650, and edited by Martin Hardie in 1919. Hardie rehearses the arguments for Norgate's authorship of that later work: the traditional ascription of the Bodleian copy of the manuscript (Tanner 326) whose preface is signed with the initials E.N., the naming of the author as E. Norgate on the Royal Society's copy of the manuscript dated 1657, the comparison of the style with that of Norgate's autograph letters and in particular the use of two Latin tags in the treatise and in one letter of Norgate's. The case is quite conclusive on the authorship of *Miniatura* (see *Miniatura*, pp.viii ff. and Harley pp.10 ff.); the problem lies in the relation between that work and the earlier *More Compendious Discourse* which has a close similarity to one section of it. The evidence points to the *More Compendious Discourse* being a condensed version of parts of an earlier working of *Miniatura*. Norgate asserts in the dedication of his work that

> At the request of a deserving friend I wrote this discourse many yeares agoe, since which time it hath broke forth and bene a wanderer and some imperfect copies have appeared under anothers name without my knowledge or consent

and there is no reason to doubt this man whom Fuller in his *History of the Worthies of England* called 'an excellent Herald by the title of [Windsor Herald] and which was the crown of all, a right honest man'. Several extant copies (e.g. Harl.6000, B.M.Add.12461, B.M.Add.34120, Harl.6376, and B.M.Add.23080) confirm Norgate's claim, being variously less full and less accurate and on occasion claimed by another author. The most scrupulous of these copies, Harl.6000, indicates the date of composition is between 1621 and 1626 and the handwriting is most probably of a date very close to the composition (see *Miniatura*, p.xiv). The hand of the *More Compendious Discourse* in the Edinburgh manuscript is according to Sir George Warner (quoted in Norman, p.5) 'a little earlier than the middle of the seventeenth century,' a dating with which we are in agreement. Philip Norman suggested that the *More Compendious Discourse* was by Hilliard and was 'put together by a personal friend, perhaps by his own son who was a limner, from information furnished by him,' and he hypothesizes that Norgate annexed the material without acknowledgement. He further suggests that the parts of what we here print which relate to Harl.6000 are there 'generally expanded and made less rugged; the reverse process seems improbable' (p.10). The evidence, however, points the other way, to show that the *More Compendious Discourse* is derivative. Like many another copy of technical material (for example, the abbreviating of Hilliard's *Treatise* itself, referred to above), it abbreviates and condenses, omits personal and anecdotal material, cuts out aesthetic comment, and indeed confines itself to simple practical instruction; but it fails to omit consistently the connecting words and phrases which link to material only present in the longer versions; it must therefore derive from, rather than be the basis of, a longer text. A few examples will show the type. Both Harl.6000 and Add.23080 (as does the later Tann.326) have at or near the beginning a note to the effect that in the account of the colours some will be omitted as either unnecessary or dangerous or 'by reason of their cheapenes and comunitie are esteemed fitter for those wch wash prints, cards, mapps then for Limning wherof wee now speake'. From this it follows naturally to the next paragraph: 'To proceede then to beginne with the collors,' which is where the Edinburgh *More Compendious Discourse* begins, having nothing to proceed from. Similarly, having divided the colours into those that are to be ground and those that are to be washed, Harl.6000 and Add.23080 explain that they will describe the process with one colour and assume that the rest will be done likewise; having described those that shall be ground, Harl.6000 continues:

> Now concerning the collours that are to bee washed and not ground I will follow the order I observed in the former, viz.t by showing how one collour is to be prepared, to demonstrate the manner of all the rest, and soe to save vs both a doble laboure in impertinent repeticons But before I beginn I will tell you the reason whye these collours are not ground . . .

The Edinburgh manuscript (see p.98) merely says 'But befor I begine . . .', a phrase which has no logic without the missing material supplied by the other manuscripts. Equally, the end of the Edinburgh manuscript is inconclusive, ending on a conditional clause. The other manuscripts not only complete the sentence but provide a context which acknowledges Hilliard's authority for the method, and demonstrate that he was not the author of the description of it. The passage in Harl.6000, whose title of 'A Compendious Discourse . . .' is far more accurate than the abbreviated four-page version of the *More Compendious Discourse*, runs thus:

> The hayghtning must be the purest Gould (I meane Liquide) the manner of the working herof, I shall tell yow as herafter followeth, being taught me by ould Mr Hilliard. If in any of your Gould worke there bee any carving or Imbossing, and that in the brighter or lighter parts it must be sparkling or Lucent, you may very finely expresse it by raysing in those Heigh and Round places *Inoncion* or heape of the Gaule stone, or English Oker . . .

Martin Hardie was perhaps too polite in his refutation of Philip Norman's suggestions, and we ought to state emphatically our opinion that Norgate was the author of the original text from which the *More Compendious Discourse* was derived. In the fuller texts Hilliard is given sufficient acknowledgement for those recipes which derive from his personal discovery rather than from generally received practice, and we ought in turn to give acknowledgement to Norgate for his authorship of the second part of the Edinburgh text.

The Technique of Miniature Painting

The limner of the sixteenth century was far more closely involved with all the processes of his art than were most of his successors, and his meticulous care reached back into the preparation of his colours, of his painting surface and often of his brushes, though these and some colours could be bought ready made.

The brushes, or pencils as they were called, of which Norgate in the mid seventeenth century said that 'you can have noe better pencills than these what are here made at London' (*Miniatura*, p.18), were made of hair, and Blaise de Vigenère, who had seen Hilliard working, tells us that he used the hairs of a squirrel's tail. The brushes were not particularly fine, needing body to carry the colour, but had to be well graduated to the tip – 'full & thike towards the quill, & so decending to A Round and sharp point' as the *More Compendious Discourse* has it. Norgate in *Miniatura* advises that 'you are to choose of severall sizes. Some great to lay grounds are as usefull and necessary as those finer and smaller sorted, and I have ever found the middle size better then the least, especially for dead colouring and laying grounds' (p.18). This is a useful comment, for the art of limning requires a much broader technique than is commonly supposed.

The preparation of the painting surface is clearer in Norgate's version than in Hilliard's, but both stress the need for the best quality materials and the greatest niceness in their preparation. Fine card or pasteboard, often a playing card, was burnished and on it the best abortive parchment was pasted skin side outwards with finely strained starch. Finally the whole was laid parchment side down on a clean smooth grinding stone and burnished again.

Haydocke in his translation of Lomazzo's *Third Booke: of Colours* (pp.125–6) divides painting into three sorts, according to 'those moistures wherewith they are grounde', namely '*Distemper, Oile worke*, and *Frisco*'. He further subdivides Distemper into three, rather dismissing painting on walls where the colour is bound with size, and then distinguishing between 'Washing with gummed colours, but tempered very thinne and bodilesse, vsed in mappes, printed stories &c. And in Limming, where the colours are likewise mixed with gummes, but laied with a thicke body and substance: wherein much arte and neatnesse is required'. The medium of limning therefore is something between our modern notions of water-colour and gouache. The colours used were the subject of the utmost care, and Hilliard's willingness to go to great lengths to achieve the brightest results – for example in his always fresh grinding of the black for the pupil of the eye – are evident in the *Treatise*. It is worth stressing that Hilliard believed that the limner should attempt to reproduce not merely the colours but the lustre of what he represented; gold and silver would be represented by real gold and silver, and precious stones would be glazed in their proper colours.

Pigments, as is evident in the longer versions of Norgate's work but not clearly so in the *More Compendious Discourse*, were divided into two groups: those that were to be ground and those that were to be washed, since grinding would deaden the colour, to produce a fine powder. The limner would take some of this powder in a mussel shell, mix it with water and Gum Arabic as a binder, and spread it round the sides of the shell for use, soft grinding the powder afresh if this were necessary. The practice of using the colours clean and fresh is what Hilliard sees as the thing 'a limner should do' (p.73). Norgate also tells us that one could have Gum Arabic 'reduct into powder very fine and kept in a neat box of Ivory or such like. And when you temper any colour mix a little of this powder with faire water, and you will finde it to dissolve instantly. And this later was Mr Hilliards way, an excellent man, and very ingenious and in his time a great Master in this Arte' (*Miniatura*, p.11). Some colours, like the lakes, ivory black and yellow ochre, tended to crack, and sugar candy was added to the mixture to prevent this.

The painting began with the swift application of an even ground of flesh colour where the face was to be, a colour which was called 'carnation' ('flesh colour') whether the ceruse was mixed with a little red lead, or less red lead and a little massicot for a paler face, or more of both and some ochre de rouse for a browner complexion. This painting of a ground colour distinguishes the English style, for Norgate is scornful of the Italians who paint on the bare parchment in what he terms 'a slight and washing way'; and his description of the process throws an interesting light on Hilliard's practice:

> The best course therefore for you is according as Mr Hillyard and his rare disciple, Mr Isaac Olivier were wont to doe, which was to have in readiness a dozen or more Cards ready prepared, and grounds laid of severall Complexions. And when they where to drawe any picture by the Life, I have seene them choose a Card, as neare the Complexion of the party, as they could, ever remenbering to choose one rather too faire, then too broune, for in this Art of Lymning, there is noe heightning in face, but the ground it selfe serves for heightning (p.20).

The outlines were drawn lightly on this ground in lake mixed with a little of the flesh colour, or in a thin lake alone. Hilliard would then shadow by hatching with the brush; the early 17th-century practice as described by Norgate was to broadly rough in the face – what was called the dead colouring, referring not to the colour but to the preliminary quality of the sketch, lacking those touches which were finally to add the life.

Further explanation of the technique is best found in the *Treatise* itself, in Norgate's *Miniatura* and in *The English Miniature* (Yale U.P., 1981) where V. J. Murrell provides a chapter on "The Craft of the Miniaturist' (see especially pp.1–14). Mr Murrell's forthcoming edition (with Dr Jeffry Muller) of *Miniatura* and Norgate's earlier working of the material in B.M. MS. Harl.6000 will not only provide us with useful scholarly texts of those works, but should also greatly clarify our notions of painting methods and materials.

One thing more should be noted: Hilliard is very fastidious not only about the cleanliness, but also about the purity of colours, arguing that they should ideally be 'of perfection in themselves', unlike purple, for example, which he insists is a mixture and 'not a proper colour'. Even murrey, which he prefers, 'can never be so good' when it is a mixture of a lake and blue. A consequence of this belief, and one which helps make the limnings at once so bright and so innocently fresh, is that in Hilliard's work each colour is ideally shadowed not with black or with a contrasting hue (see p.79 and note 66) but with a darker tone of the same hue – 'limning is but a shadowing of the same colour your ground is of' (p.77); thus the insistence on 'shadowing yellows', 'shadowing blues' and so on, and the connection with the 'five perfect colours' of the precious stones.

A Note on Colours

Since they occur rather frequently in the text, a list of colours which require some note is gathered here. The nature and naming of colours are subject to sometimes subtle and sometimes quite major changes, and there is no room here to go to the lengths necessary to follow all the intricacies of change and argument; these may be found in Dr R.D. Harley's invaluable *Artists' Pigments c.1600–1835* (1970), from which much of the following information is derived. Information followed by the initials V.J.M. has been generously supplied by Mr V.J. Murrell.

asphaltum — a dark brown shadowing colour. Asphaltum (presumably what is meant by *spalte*) is 'a very strange pigment to use in water colour. However, it should be remembered that water colour *pigments* should *not* be soluble in water and, given adequate preparation, there is no reason why asphaltum should not have been used.' (V.J.M.).

bice — blue, but sometimes green or tending to green. 'One should distinguish between blue bice (azurite) and green bice (malachite). As minerals they are often discovered in close proximity and it is this that can cause variations in the colour of blue bice.' (V.J.M.). The minerals would be crushed and washed; grinding would tend to deaden the colour.

carnation — not a colour in its own right, but the term for flesh tints mixed from ceruse and red lead, sometimes with massicot and/or ochre de rouse.

ceder green — green made from chrysocolla (copper silicate), the name deriving from *solder green* from its use as an adhesive for gold. Hilliard seems to give contradictory instructions in that under 'Colours' he includes this in a list to be softly ground, while under 'Greens' he includes it in a list which needs washing and not grinding. Norgate shows that the latter is the correct advice, as with bice.

ceruse white. Since Hilliard lists both ceruse and lead white, they are not synonymous as they were for later seventeenth-century writers. Hilliard's carnations are non-metallic. 'This is deduced from a wide selection of X-radiographs of Hilliard miniatures. Lead white has a relatively high atomic weight and absorbs X-rays, showing as a white area on the X-ray film. It is remarkable that although lead white can be clearly seen to have been used on the costumes, the carnations appear as black areas, suggesting the use of the chalk/alum mixture which is mentioned in several MSS of the period.' (V.J.M.)

earth of Cologne deep brown, derived from deposits of lignite or peat.

English ochre yellow. Iron oxide found naturally occurring in various shades from yellow through to brown.

fleur-de-lys green. The petals of the flower 'were bruised and soaked in water to extract a dye which was then precipitated on alum' (Harley). The method similar to preparing yellow from white roses (p.75).

florey flower of woad, or indigo, made from the foam on the dye vats in which woad or indigo was being used. A dark blue.

gall-stone dark yellow, used as a shadowing yellow, and in painting gold, made from crushed ox-gall.

India Lake dark red, made from lac i.e. the females, eggs and the exudation surrounding them, of the insect *Coccus lacca*. Both the name and the make-up of lakes in general are changeable and best studied at length in Harley and Thompson.

indigo — deep blue, made from the leaves of *Indigofera.*

lake — as a colour, red; but also used by Hilliard as a type of pigment made from lac (see *India lake*), as in 'murrey . . . must be a lake of himself'. (p.73).

litmus — blue. Hilliard's dismissal of this colour for limning (though he mentions it as a shadowing blue) presumably rests not only on its smell as he suggests, but also on its well-known tendency to revert to red, which is modified by the suggested mixing with lye.

massicot — yellow of various tones, made from lead and tin.

murrey — mulberry-coloured, a colour name not attached to a particular pigment.

ochre de rouse — a dark yellow-brown iron oxide.

orpiment — brilliant yellow made of sulphide of arsenic generally disliked for its poisonous qualities and its incompatibility with some other colours.

pansy green — green extracted from the petals of pansies or violets in the same way as fleur-de-lys green.

pink — a yellow lake, tending to green, often used mixed with bice to form a deep green.

red lead — the rather orange tetroxide of lead, whose Latin name *minium* provided the name miniaturists for those rubricators and illuminators who used it.

sap green — a dark yellow-green used for shadowing, made from ripe buckthorn berries.

smalt	blue, the best said to be deep violet-blue, made from pulverised glass which had been coloured by oxide of cobalt.
Terra de Collona	see earth of Cologne.
ultramarine	blue made of lapis lazuli, the costliest of pigments.
umber	probably the red-brown burnt umber, an earth containing iron oxide and manganese dioxide.
verdigris	a green with a bluish tinge, an acetate of copper.
verditer	'Verditers (either blue or green) are *artificial* copper carbonates, as opposed to their natural counterparts azurite and malachite (blue and green bice).' (V.J.M.).
vermilion	red mercuric sulphide.
white lead	probably lead carbonate, but possibly lead acetate, although gentle roasting in the sun could have formed lead carbonate from the acetate.

A Note on the Text

Philip Norman's edition is a compromise between accuracy and readability, retaining the original spelling but not capitalisation and italicisation, and imposing some shape (and indeed some readings) with punctuation and paragraphing. Indeed, it is difficult to see how one could satisfy all demands with one text. We have been fortunate, therefore, to meet with a publisher who will give us the scope to publish two versions of the text side by side. The first is an exact transcript of the manuscript, simply reproducing what is there, warts and all, without tedious repetitions of *sic* at every turn; we have not expanded contractions (though we have been unable to set superscript endings above the line) or altered what seemed clearly to be mistakes, though we have silently restored letters lost in the guttering or at the edge of the page, if the nature of the missing letters was not in doubt. The second version is thus allowed to be a modernisation for reading purposes, any doubtful readings in which can immediately be checked against the original; any inserted readings, variants, hypothetical emendations could be made in this version without the danger of obscuring the original which is there for all to see. We have used Vertue's version, which is probably a transcription, of the material torn from the recto of the first page (see p.42) but have had to attempt to reconstitute the material from the verso (see pp.44 and 45) which Vertue did not transcribe. We have tried to reproduce the scribe's attempts at italic, but have judged from general appearance when the italic and secretary hand forms occurred indiscriminately within a single word. We did not go so far as to translate words or substitute modern usages, since that would spoil the flavour of what is, when seen clearly, not only an interesting work on art but also an accomplished and lively piece of prose.

A TREATISE
CONCERNING THE ARTE OF LIMNING

writ by N. HILLIARD

at the request of R. Haydocke who publisht in English a translation of Paulo Lomazzo on Painting 1598

[Of Precepts & directions for ye] arte of paintinge I will saye littel In so much as *Paulo Lomatzo* [& others hath excellently & learnedly spo]ken therof, as is well knowen to the learned & better sorte [who are conversant with those] auhtors, But only intending to teache the arte of limning, and the [True method leading th]ervnto, as also to shewe who are fittest to be practisers [thereof, for whom only] let it suffice that I intend my whole discourse that way:

[Amongst ye an]cient *Romans* in time past forbad that any should [shoud be taught the Ar]te of *Painting* saue gentelmen only, I coniecture they Did it [upon judgment of th]is ground, as thinking that noe man vsing the same to get his liuing [by, if he was a needy] *Artificer* could haue the patience or leasure to performe any [exact true & rare] peece of worke, but men Ingeniously borne, and of sufficient means [not subject to] . . . se comon cares of the world for food and garment, moued with [emulation a]nd desier therof, would doe theier vtermost best not respecting the [profitt o]r the lenght of time nor permit any vnworthy vnworthy worke to be pubblished vnder their name to comon view, but deface it againe rather and neuer leaue till some excelent pece of Arte were by him or them performed worthy of some comendations, by Reason wherof it was no wonder that the most excelent nation and the greatest witts of the world then brought forth the most rare workes in painting that euer weare, it must needs be granted then for euer, and like as one good workman then mad an other, so one bocher nowe adaies maketh many and they increasse so fast that good workmen giue ouer to vsse their best skill, for all men cary one price, now therfor I wish it weare so that none should medle with limning, but gentelmen alone, for that it is a kind of gentill painting of lesse subiection then any other for one may leaue when hee will, his coullers nor his work taketh any harme by it, Morouer it is secreat a man may vsse it and scarsly be perseaued of his owne folke it is sweet and cleanly to vsse, and it is a thing apart from all other *Painting* or *drawing* and tendeth not to comon mens vsse, either for furnishing of Howsses, or any patternes for tapistries, or *Building*, or any other worke whatsoeuer, and yet it excelleth all other *Painting* what soeuer in sondry points, in giuing the true lustur to pearle and precious stone, and worketh the metals *Gold* or *Siluer* with themselfes which so enricheth and innobleth the worke that it seemeth to be the thinge it sefe euen the worke of god and not of man, beining fittest for the decking of princes bookes or to put in Ieuuells of gould and for the

Of precepts and directions for the[17] art of painting I will say little, insomuch as Paolo Lomazzo[18] and others have excellently and learnedly spoken thereof, as is well known to the learned and better sort who are conversant with those authors; but only intending to teach the art of limning, and the true method leading thereunto, as also to show who are fittest to be practicers thereof, for whom only let it suffice that I intend my whole discourse that way.

The ancient Romans in time past forbade that any should be taught the art of painting, save gentlemen only. I conjecture they did it upon judgment of this ground: as thinking that no man using the same to get his living by, if he was a needy artificer, could have the patience or leisure to perform any exact, true and rare piece of work; but men ingeniously born, and of sufficient means, not subject to those common cares of the world for food and garment, moved with emulation and desire thereof, would do their uttermost best, not respecting the profit or the length of time; nor permit any unworthy work to be published under their name to common view, but deface it again rather, and never leave till some excellent piece of art were by him or them performed worthy of some commendations. By reason whereof it was no wonder that the most excellent nation and the greatest wits of the world then brought forth the most rare works in painting that ever were; it must needs be granted then for ever. And like as one good workman then made another, so one botcher nowadays maketh many, and they increase so fast that good workmen give over to use their best skill, for all men carry one price.

Now, therefore, I wish it were so that none should meddle with limning but gentlemen alone, for that it is a kind of gentle painting, of less subjection than any other; for one may leave when he will, his colours nor his work taketh any harm by it. Moreover, it is secret: a man may use it, and scarcely be perceived of his own folk. It is sweet and cleanly to use, and it is a thing apart from all other painting or drawing, and tendeth not to common men's use, either for furnishing of houses, or any patterns for tapestries, or building, or any other work whatsoever. And yet it excelleth all other painting whatsoever in sundry points, in giving the true lustre to pearl and precious stone, and worketh the metals gold or silver with themselves, which so enricheth and ennobleth the work that it seemeth to be the thing itself, even the work of God and not of man: being fittest for the decking of princes' books, or to put in jewels of gold,

imitation of the purest flowers and most beautifull creaturs in the finest and purest coullers which are chargable and is for the seruice of noble persons very meet in small voloms in priuat maner for theem to haue the *Portraits* and pictures of themselues (f. 1v.)
their peers, or any other forraine . . .
them, And this is a worke which of . . .
owne pressence for the most part of th . . .
uenient that they be gentelmen of g . . .
of abbillity, or mad by princes fee, a . . .
to giue such seemly atendance one *Pr* . . .
Ecclesiasticus Royall presence, Seest thou not that th . . .
in theire bussines stand before *Prince* . . .
mon peeople, But god the aughter of wisdo . . .
all good guifts and goodnes, he giueth *Gæntilit* . . .
rayseth man to reputation by diuers mean . . .
he called *Basaleel* And *Ahohas* by name and . . .
wissdome, skill, and vnderstanding, without any te . . .
of his own guift and grace receued . . .
himself to be cuninge in all fine and curious . . .
silke, in painting, in setting of precious stones in gould . . .
the text sayeth he filled them with the sperit of god to . . .
such works, being men before brought up but in s . . .
of brickes in captiuitye they and their Ancestors . . .
generations: Heer is a kind of true gentility when god caleth and doubtles though gentelmen be the metest for this gentill caling or practice, yet not all but naturall aptnes is to be chossen and prefered, for not euery gentelman is so gentel sperited as som others are, Let vs therfore honore and prefferre the election of god in all vocations and degrees, and suerly he is a very wisse man that can find out the naturall Inclination of his childeren, in due time, and soe applie him that waye which nature most inclineth him, if it be good or may be made good, as it may be vssed, though in childhood abussed, and as for an naturall aptnes of or to painting after the liffe thosse surly which haue such a guift of god ought to reioyce with humble thankfulnes and to be very wary and temperat in diet and other gouerment, least it be sone taken from them againe by some sudaine mischance, or by their euell coustomes, their sight, or stedines of hand decay, then this exortation giue I more, that he be diligent, yea euer diligent, and put his whole vttermost and best endeauors to exceell all other, for a stronge man that putteth not

and for the imitation of the purest flowers and most beautiful creatures in the finest and purest colours which are chargeable;[19] and is for the service of noble persons very meet, in small volumes, in private manner, for them to have the portraits and pictures of themselves, their peers, or any other foreign persons which are of interest to them. And this is a work which of necessity requireth the party's own presence for the most part of the time, and so it is convenient that they be gentlemen of good parts and ingenuity, either of ability, or made by prince's fee able so to carry themselves as to give such seemly attendance on princes as shall not offend their royal presence. Seest thou not that these men, then, must often in their business stand before princes, though they be born but common people? But God, the author of wisdom and the giver of all good gifts and goodness, He giveth gentility to divers persons, and raiseth man to reputation by divers means: we read that He called Bezaleel and Aholiab by name, and filled them with wisdom, skill and understanding, without any teaching, but only of His own gift and grace received. He taught them Himself to be cunning in all fine and curious work, in embroidering in silk, in painting, in setting of precious stones in gold, and carving of wood. The text sayeth He filled them with the spirit of God to devise cunningly in such works, being men before brought up but in slavery and making of bricks in captivity, they and their ancestors for many generations.

Ecclesiasticus[20]

Here is a kind of true gentility, when God calleth: and doubtless though gentlemen be the meetest for this gentle calling or practice, yet not all; but natural aptness is to be chosen and preferred, for not every gentleman is so gentle spirited as some others are. Let us therefore honour and prefer the election of God in all vocations and degrees: and surely he is a very wise man that can find out the natural inclinations of his children in due time, and so apply him that way which nature most inclineth him, if it be good, or may be made good; as it may be used, though in childhood abused. And as for a natural aptness of or to painting after the life, those surely which have such a gift of God ought to rejoice with humble thankfulness, and to be very wary and temperate in diet and other government, lest it be soon taken from them again by some sudden mischance, or, by their evil customs, their sight or steadiness of hand decay.

Then this exhortation give I more, that he be diligent, yea ever diligent, and put his whole uttermost and best endeavours to excel all others; for a strong man that putteth not forth his strength is often foiled by a weaker forth his strenght, is often foyled by weaker, and the most perfect and cuningest, must doe the same diligence, or rather more, to effect and performe his worke, then hee did at the first in larninge, for it can not be sayd that a man be he neuer so cunning by teaching or naturall Inclination, yet it will growe out of him as haire out of the head, or fall from him whether he will or no, but with great labour, and this comfort shall he haue then aboue others, euen an heauen of Ioy in his hart to behould his own well doings remaining to his credit for euer, yea if Men of worth did knowe what delight it (f.*2r.*) breedeth, how it remoueth mallancoly, auodeth euell occasions, putteth passions of sorrowe or greefe awaye, cureth rage, and shortneth the times, they would neuer leaue till they had attained in some good meassur, A more then comfort maie he haue, both praysse and euen honor in the sight of men liuing, and fame for euer after, And *Princes* comonly giue them competent meanes, by which not their workmen soe much as themselues ar eternized, and famously remembred as the nuresses of vertue and Arts, wherfore it is truly written *Honos alit artes*, and many noble and honorable perssons haue bine practizers themselues of the art of painting, as *Lomatius* very learnedly and truly hath in order repeated and some haue counted themselues the greater therby as the famous and victorious *Roman Quintus ffabius* added as an honnore vnto his tytle to be called *Quintus ffabius Pictor*,/. And *Pamitius* recokoning vp the famous barons and worthy perssons which weear attendant on the emperour *Marcus Aurelius*, remembreth, and shortly amonge them this principal *Painter*: neuertheles if a man be so indued by nature and liue in time of trouble, and vnder a sauage gouerment, wherin arts be not esteemed, and himselfe but of small meanes: woe be vnto him as vnto an vntimly *Birth*: for of mine owne knowlege it hath mad poure men poorer, as among others many, the most rare *Englishe Drawer* of Story works in black and white, *Iohn Bossam*, for one of his skill worthy to haue bene *Sergant Painter* to any king or *Emperour*, whose work in that kind are comperable with the best whatsoeuer in cloathe in distemper cullors for whit and black, whoe being very poore, and belyke wanting to buy faier cullors, wrought therfore for the most part in whit and black, and growing yet poorer by charge of childeren &tc, gaue painting cleane ouer: But being a very faier conditioned zealious and godly persson, grewe into a loue of gods deuine seruice vpon the liberty of the gosspell at the coming in of quene Elizath, and became a reading *Minister*, vnly vnfortunat and the most perfect and cunningest must do the same diligence, or rather more, to effect and perform his work, than he did at the first in learning. For it cannot be said that a man, be he never so cunning by teaching or natural inclination, yet it will grow out of him as hair out of the head, or fall from him whether he will or no, but with great labour; and this comfort shall he have then above others, even a heaven of joy in his heart to behold his own well doings remaining to his credit forever. Yea, if men of worth did know what delight it breedeth, how it removeth melancholy, avoideth evil occasions, putteth passions of sorrow or grief away, cureth rage, and shortneth the times, they would never leave till they had attained in some good measure. A more than comfort may he have, both praise and even honour in the sight of men living, and fame for ever after; and princes commonly give them competent means, by which not their workmen so much as themselves are eternized, and famously remembered as the nurses of virtue and arts. Wherefore it is truly written, *Honos alit artes*;[21] and many noble and honourable persons have been practicers themselves of the art of painting, as Lomazzo very learnedly and truly hath in order repeated.[22] And some have counted themselves the greater thereby, as the famous and victorious Roman, Quintus Fabius,[23] added it as an honour unto his title to be called Quintus Fabius Pictor; and Pamitius,[24] reckoning up the famous barons and worthy persons which were attendant on the emperor Marcus Aurelius, remembreth, and shortly among them, his principal painter.

Nevertheless, if a man be so endued by nature, and live in time of trouble, and under a savage government wherein arts be not esteemed, and himself but of small means, woe be unto him as unto an untimely birth! For of mine own knowledge it hath made poor men poorer, as among others (many) the most rare English drawer of story works[25] in black and white, John Bossam;[26] one for his skill worthy to have been Serjeant Painter to any king or emperor, whose works in that kind are comparable with the best whatsoever, in cloth, in distemper colours, or white and black. Who, being very poor, and belike wanting to buy fair colours, wrought therefore for the most part in white and black; and growing yet poorer by charge of children etc., gave painting clean over; but being a very fair conditioned, zealous and godly person, grew into a love of God's divine service, upon the liberty of the gospel at the coming in of Queen Elizabeth, and became a reading minister: only unfortunate becasse he was english borne, for euen the strangers would otherwisse haue set him vpp, Heer must I needs incert a word or two in honore and praisse of the renowned and mighty *King Henry the eight* a *Prince* of exquisit Iugment: and Royall bounty, soe that of cuning Stranger euen the best resorted vnto him, and remoued from other courts to his, Amongst whom came the most excelent painter and limner *Haunce Holbean*, the greatest Mter truly in both thosse arts after the liffe that euer was, so cuning in both to gether, and the neatest, and thewithall a good inuentor soe compleat for all three, as I neuer hard of any better then hee yet had the King in wages for *Limning* diuers others, but *Holbeans* maner of *Limning* I haue euer Imitated, and howld it for the best, by Reason that of truth all the rare siences, especially the arts of *Caruing*, *Painting*, *Gouldsmiths*, *Imbroderers*, together with the most of all the liberall siences came first vnto vs from the Strangers, and generally they are the best, and most in number, I hard kimsard the great french poet on a time say, that the Ilands indeed seldome bring forth any cunning Man, but when they doe, it is in high perfection so then I (f.2*v*.) hope I hope there maie come out of this ower land such a one, this being the greatest and most famous Iland of *Europe*: the most excelent *Albert Dure* was borne in *Germany*, a part of the greatest Mayneland in *Europe*, which breedeth or might breed more then a hundred workmen for vs one, this *Albert* being as exquisite and perfect and pfect a *Painter*, and Mtr in the art of *Grauing* on *Copper* as euer was since the world begane, (that by many works exstant appeareth) and which also hath written the best and most rulles of and for painting and grauing hethervnto of any maister vntill *Paulo Lamatio*, which Rulles of *Albert* for the most part ar hard to be remembred, and tedious to be foloued of Painters, being so ful of diuisons, but very fittable for caruers and masons, for *architects* and fortifications, and all which drawing is the enterance the very high waye and foundation, he dowtlesse had opinion that not in hast or short time his better shold arisse, wherfor as it hath bene vnto me credabelly Reported, he resserued some plats of his owne grauing for printing, which he gaue vnto the city of *Norenbourgh* wherof he was a worthy counselor which he kept fo a time, rquiring of them by his will and testament that thosse plats should not be printed, vntill one hundred yeares after his weare fully expired and past, that he might then arisse againe after a houndred years to his greater fame, if in the meane time he wear not excelled by any other, which plats ar yet

Albert Duer

because he was English born, for even the strangers would otherwise have set him up.

Here must I needs insert a word or two in honour and praise of the renowned and mighty King Henry the eighth, a prince of exquisite judgment and royal bounty, so that of cunning strangers even the best resorted unto him and removed from other courts to his; amongst whom came the most excellent painter and limner, Hans Holbein, the greatest master truly in both those arts after the life that ever was: so cunning in both together, and the neatest, and therewithall a good inventor; so complete for all three as I never heard of any better than he. Yet had the King in wages for limning divers others; but Holbein's manner of limning I have ever imitated, and hold it for the best, by reason that of truth all the rare sciences, especially the arts of carving, painting, goldsmiths, embroiderers, together with the most of all the liberal sciences, came first unto us from the strangers, and generally they are the best and most in number. I heard Ronsard the great French poet on a time say that the islands indeed seldom bring forth any cunning man, but when they do it is in high perfection; so then I hope there may come out of this our land such a one, this being the greatest and most famous island of Europe.

Albert Dürer

The most excellent Albert Dürer was born in Germany, a part of the greatest mainland in Europe, which breedeth, or might breed, more than a hundred workmen for us one; this Albert being as exquisite and perfect a painter and master in the art of engraving on copper as ever was since the world began, that by many works extant appeareth; and which also hath written the best and most rules of and for painting and engraving hitherunto of any master until Paolo Lomazzo.[27] Which rules of Albert for the most part are hard to be remembered, and tedious to be followed of painters, being so full of divisions; but very fittable for carvers and masons, for architects and builders of fortifications, and all to which drawing is the entrance, the very highway and foundation. He doubtless had opinion that not in haste or short time his better should arise; wherefore, as it hath been unto me credibly reported, he reserved some plates of his own engraving for printing, which he gave unto the city of Nuremberg, whereof he was a worthy councillor, which he kept for a time, requiring of them by his will and testament that those plates should not be printed until one hundred years after his death were fully expired and past, that he might then arise again after a hundred years to his greater fame, if in the meantime he were not excelled by any other: which plates reserued vnprinted to his great credit, and which in due time to his greater fame will doubtles be deuolged, yet hath ther beene diuers excelent persons of that nation and of Italy, france, and the lowe countries also, wherof *Hendrick Goltzius*, aproched *Albertus* very neer, most admirably imitating him, and *Lucas of Leyden*, also, in their seuerall handling the grauer, which he hath done in sertaine peces to showe what he could doe if he list, but he afecteth an other maner of line, which is swifter acording to his spirit, and doubtles very excelent, and most folowed, that Man is worthy to be remembred in bouck to posterity, which excelleth all men in that age, in that matter, wherof he is professer, *Albertus Dure* was both inuentor and grauer, as few of the rest of the grauers are, a double honnor to him, nowe the reasson why the rules of *Alberte*, serue more the caruer then the *Painter* is becausse he discribeth and deuideth the ppeortion or of parts of men, like as of pillors or such other things, by measures of inches in lenght, breadth, thiknes, and circumference, which measures serue not, nor can howld in painting, for as *Lamatzo* truly speaketh in the eleuenth chapter of *Opticio*, you cannot measure any part of yr pictures by his true *superficious*, Because painting perspectiue, and forshortning (f.3*r*.) of lines, with due shadoing acording to the rule of the eye, by falshood to expresse truth in very cunning of line, and true obseruation of shadoing, especially in human shapes, as the figure, lieth boweth, or standeth, and is situated, or is, and aptly shalbe placed to deceaue the eye, for perspectiue, to define it brefly, is an art taken from, or by, the efect, or Iugment of the eye, for a man to express, anything in shortned lines, and shadowes, to deseaue bothe the vnderstanding and the eye, this cassed the famous and eloquent *cissero* to say, O how many things doe painters see in highning or lightning, and shadowing, which wee deserne not, and heer I enter myne opinion conserning the question, whether of the two arts is the most worthy, *Painting, or Carueing*, I say if they be tow arts, painting is the worthier, as in the last leafe I hope I shall proue suficiently, againe I will Doe Cuning *Albert* no wronge, but Right, dowbtles he was the most exquisite man that euer leaft vs lines to vieue, for true delination, the most perfect shadower that euer graued in metall, for true shadowes, and one of the best and truest in his perspectiue, but yet it must be thought or rather heeld for sertaine by reason that he was no great traueller, that he neuer sawe thosse faier creatures that the Italions had seene, as *Rousso*, *Raphel*, and *Lambertus Swauius* &c /

are yet reserved unprinted, to his great credit, and which in due time to his greater fame will doubtless be divulged.

Yet have there been divers excellent persons of that nation, and of Italy, France and the Low Countries also, whereof Hendrick Goltzius[28] approached Albertus very near, most admirably imitating him and Lucas of Leyden[29] also, in their several handling of the graver,[30] which he hath done in certain pieces to show what he could do if he list; but he affecteth another manner of line, which is swifter according to his spirit, and doubtless very excellent, and most followed. That man is worthy to be remembered in books to posterity, which excelleth all men in that age in that matter wherof he is professor: Albertus Durer was both inventor and engraver, as few of the rest of the engravers are; a double honour to him.

Now the reason why the rules of Albert serve more the carver than the painter is because he describeth and divideth the proportions of parts of men, like as of pillars or such other things, by measure of inches in length, breadth, thickness and circumference: which measures serve not, nor can hold in painting, for as Lomazzo truly speaketh in the eleventh chapter, *Of Optica*, 'you cannot measure any part of your picture by his true superfices,'[31] because painting perspective and foreshortening of lines, with due shadowing, according to the rule of the eye, worketh by falsehood to express truth in very cunning of line and true observation of shadowing – especially in human shapes, as the figure lieth, boweth, or standeth, and is situated, or is and aptly shall be placed to deceive the eye. For perspective, to define it briefly, is an art taken from or by the effect or judgment of the eye, for a man to express anything in shortened lines and shadows, to deceive both the understanding and the eye. This caused the famous and eloquent Cicero to say, 'O how many things do painters see in heightening or lightening and shadowing, which we discern not.'[32]

And here I enter my opinion concerning the question which of the two arts is the most worthy, painting or carving: I say (if they be two arts) painting is the worthier, as in the last leaf I hope I shall prove sufficiently.[33] Again, I will do cunning Albert no wrong, but right: doubtless he was the most exquisite man that ever left us lines to view, for true delineation; the most perfect shadower that ever engraved in metal, for true shadows; and one of the best and truest in his perspective. But yet it must be thought, or rather held for certain (by reason that he was no great traveller),[34] that he never saw those fair creatures that the Italians had seen, as Rosso,[35] Raphael, and Lambertus Suavius,[36] etc. For besides a for besides a certaine true proportion, some of thirs doe excell his in kind of beautifulnes, and sperit in the linament and Iesture, with delicacye of feature, and limes hands and feet, surpassing all other portractures of the duch whatsoeuer, yea euen nature it self, except in very few which rare beautys are euen as the diamons are found amongst the sauage indians, more commonly found in this yle of england then else where, such surely as art euer must giue place vnto I saye not for the face only, but euery part, for euen the hand, and fooet, excelleth all pictures, that yet I euer sawe / this moued a sertaine *Pope* to say that england was Rightly called *Anglia* of *Angely*, as the country of *Angels*, god grant it, and now to the matter for precepts for Obseruations, ore directions to the art of limning, which yo requier, as breefly and ar plainly as I can, Concerning the best waye and meanes to practice and ataine to skill in *Limning*, in a word befor I exhorted such to temperance, I meane sleepe not much, wacth not much, eat not much, sit not long, vsse not violent excersize in sports, nor eanest for yr recreation / but dancing or bowling, or littel of either, / them the fierst and cheefest precepts which I giue, is cleanlynes, and therfor fittest for gentelmen, that the praticer of *Limning* be presizly pure and klenly in all his doings, as in grinding his coulers in place wher ther is neither dust nor smoake, the watter wel chossen or distilled most pure, as the watter distilled frome the watter of some clear spring, or frome black cherize which is the Cleanest (f.3*v.*) that euer I could find, and keepeth longest sweet and cleare, the goume to be *Goume Aarabeeke*, of the whitest and briclest broken into whit pouder, one a faire and cleare grinding stone, and whit suger candy in like sort to be keept dry in boxes of *Iuory* the grinding stone of fine *Cristall*, *Serpentine*, *Iasper*, *or Hard Porfory*, at the least let yr aparell be silke, such as sheadeth lest dust *Dust* or haires weare nothing straight, beware yo tuch not yr worke with yr fingers, or any hard thing, but with a cleane pencel brush it, or with a whit feather, neither breath one it, especially in could weather, take heed of the dandrawe of the head sheading from the haire, and of speaking ouer yr worke for sparkling, for the least sparkling of spettel, will neuer be holpen if it light in the face or any part of the naked, the second Rulle is much like the first, and conserning the light and place wher yo worke in, let yr light be nothword, somwhat toward the east which comonly is without sune, *Shininge* in. on only light great and faire let it be, and without impeachment, or reflections, of walls, or trees, a free sky

England for beautifull cratures

Rule 2°

certain true proportion, some of theirs do excel his in kind of beautifulness and spirit in the lineament and gesture, with delicacy of feature and limbs, hands and feet, surpassing all other portraitures of the Dutch whatsoever – yea, even nature itself, except in very few; which rare beauties are, even as the diamonds are found among the savage Indians, more commonly found in this isle of England than elsewhere, such surely as art ever must give place unto. I say not for the face only, but every part; for even the hand and foot excelleth all pictures that yet I ever saw. This moved a certain Pope to say that England was rightly called Anglia, of *angeli*, as the country of angels: God grant it.

England for beautiful creatures

And now to the matter for precepts, for observations or directions to the art of limning, which you require as briefly and as plainly as I can, concerning the best way and means to practice and attain to skill in limning. In a word before, I exhorted such to temperance; I mean sleep not much, watch not much, eat not much, sit not long, use not violent exercise in sports, nor earnest for your recreation, but dancing or bowling or little of either. Then the first and chiefest precept which I give is cleanliness, and therefore fittest for gentlemen; that the practicer of limning be precisely pure and cleanly in all his doings: as in grinding his colours in place where there is neither dust nor smoke; the water well chosen, or distilled most pure, as the water distilled from the water of some clear spring, or from black cherries, which is the cleanest that ever I could find, and keepeth longest sweet and clear; the gum to be gum arabic of the whitest and brittlest, broken into white powder on a fair and clean grinding stone; and white sugar candy in like sort to be kept dry in boxes of ivory; the grinding stone of fine crystal, serpentine, jasper or hard porphyry at the least. Let your apparel be silk, such as sheddeth least dust or hairs; wear nothing straight.[37] Beware you touch not your work with your fingers, or any hard thing, but with a clean pencil[38] brush it, or with a white feather; neither breathe on it, especially in cold weather. Take heed of the dandruff of the head shedding from the hair, and of speaking over your work for sparkling, for the least sparkling of spittle will never be helped if it light in the face, or any part of the naked.[39]

The second rule is much like the first, and concerns the light and place where you work in. Let your light be northward, somewhat toward the east, which commonly is without sun shining in. One only light: great and fair let it be, and without impeachment, or reflections of walls or trees, light the dieper the window and farer, the better, and no by window, but a cleare story in a place wher neither dust, smoak, noisse, nor steanche may ofend, a good painter hath tender sences, quiet and apt, and the culers them sellues may not endure some ayers, especially in the sulfirous ayre of seacole, and the guilding of Gowld-smithes, sweet odors comforteth the braine and openeth the vnderstanding, augmenting the delight in *Limning*, *Discret* talke or reading, quiet merth or musike ofendeth not, but shortneth the time, and quickneth the sperit both in the drawer, and he which is drawne, also in any wisse auoyd anger, shut out questioners or busi fingers, all theesse things may be hadd, and this authority may best be vssed by gentelmen, therfor in truth the *Art* fitteth for them, now

of Painting knowe that all *Painting* imitateth nature, or the life in euery thinge, it resembleth so fare forth as the *Painters* memory or skill can serue him to expresse, in all or any maner of story worke, embleme, empresse, or other deuice whatsoeuer, but of all things the perfection is to imitate the face of man kind, or the hardest part of it, and which carieth most prayesse and comendations, and which indeed one should not atempt vntill he weare metly good in story worke, soe neare and so weel after the life, as that not only the party in all liknes for fauor and complection is or may be very well resembled but euen his best graces and countenance notabelly expressed, for ther is no person but hath variety of looks, and countenance, as well ilbecoming as pleassing or delighting, wherof it is not amis to say somwhat in briffe tuching this point, leauing the better handling therof to better wits, wherin the best shall find infinite arguments, right pleasant (f.4*r*.) to discoure vppon and herof it cometh that men commonly say of some drawer, he maketh very like, but better yet for them then the party is in deed, and of some other they also say he maketh very faier, but worsse fauored in the comlynes and beauty of the face, therfor which giueth vs such pleasinge, and feedeth soe wonderful ower afection, mor then all the worlds
1 treassure, it consisteth in three points, the first and least is the faire and beautiful couler or complection which euen a fare of, as neare
2 is pleassing greatly all behoulders, the next and greater part is the good proportion somtime called fauore, wherof ouer deuine part vppon nearer viw, by an admirable instint of nature, Iugeth generally, both in wisse, and foolish, yong, or owld, learned, and simpel, and knoweth by nature without rule or reasson for it, whoe
3 is well proportioned or well fauored, &c but the third part &c

a free skylight; the deeper the window and fairer, the better; and no by-window, but a clerestory in a place where neither dust, smoke, noise nor stench may offend. A good painter hath tender senses, quiet and apt; and the colours themselves may not endure some airs, especially in the sulphurous air of seacoal, and the gilding of goldsmiths. Sweet odours comfort the brain, and open the understanding, augmenting the delight in limning. Discreet talk or reading, quiet mirth or music, offend not, but shorten the time and quicken the spirit, both in the drawer and he which is drawn. Also in any wise avoid anger, shut out questioners or busy fingers. All these things may be had, and this authority may best be used, by gentlemen; therefore in truth the art fitteth for them.

Of painting

Now know that all painting imitateth nature, or the life; in everything, it resembleth so far forth as the painter's memory or skill can serve him to express, in all or any manner of story work, emblem, impresa,[40] or other device whatsoever. But of all things, the perfection is to imitate the face of mankind (or the hardest part of it, and which carrieth most praise and commendations, and which indeed one should not attempt until he were meetly good in story work) so near and so well after the life as that not only the party in all likeness for favour and complexion is, or may be, very well resembled, but even his best graces and countenance notably expressed; for there is no person but hath variety of looks and countenance, as well ill-becoming as pleasing or delighting.

Whereof it is not amiss to say something in brief touching this point, leaving the better handling thereof to better wits, wherein the best shall find infinite arguments, right pleasant to discourse upon. And hereof it cometh that men commonly say of some drawer, 'He maketh very like, but better yet for them, than the party is indeed'; and of some other they also say, 'He maketh very fair, but worse favoured'. The comeliness and beauty of the face therefore, which giveth us such pleasing, and feedeth so wonderfully our affection, more than all the world's treasure, it consisteth in three points: the first, and least, is the fair and beautiful colour or complexion, which even afar off, as near, is pleasing greatly to all beholders. The next, and greater part, is the good proportion, sometimes called favour,[41] whereof our divine part upon nearer view, by an admirable instinct of nature judgeth generally, both in wise and foolish, young or old, learned and simple, and knoweth by nature, without rule or reason for it, who is well-proportioned or well-favoured, etc. But the greatest of all is the grace in countenance, by which the afections apeare, which can neither be weel vssed nor well Iuged of but of the wisser sort, and this princepall part of the beauty a good painter hath skill of and should diligently noet, wherfor it behoueth that he be in hart wisse, as it will hardly faill that he shalbe amorous, (and therfore fittest for gen̄t:) for whoe seeth an exelent precious stone, or diserneth an exelent peece of musike with skill indeede, and is not moued aboue others with an amorous Ioye and contentment then the vulger, howbeit *gent* or *vulgar* wee are all generally commanded to turne awaye ouer eyes frome beauty of humayne shape, least it inflame the mind, howe then the curious drawer wach, and as it catch thosse louely graces wittye smilings, and thosse stolne glances wch sudainely like lighting passe and another Countenance taketh place except hee behould, and very well noate, and Conceit to lyke, soe that he can hardly take them truly, and expresse them well, wthout an affectionate good Iugment, and wthout blasting his younge and simpel hart, although (in pleassing admiration) he be very serious bussied, so hard a matter he hath in hand, calling thosse graces one by one to theire due places, notinge howe in smilling howe the eye changeth and naroweth, houlding the sight yust between the lides as a center, howe the mouth alittel extendeth both ends of the line vpwards, the Cheekes rayse themselues to the eye wards, the nosterels play and are more open, the vaines in the tempel appeare more, and the cullour by degrees increaseth, the necke commonly erecteth it selfe, the eye browes make the straighter arches, and the forhead casteth it selfe in to a plaine as it wear for peace and loue to walke vppon, in like sort countenances of wroth, of feare, or of sorowe, haue their seuerall alterance of the face, and fare according to the mind is affected, may be many faces, some louly, some loathsom, some graue and wisse, some foolish and wanton, some proude and audatious, some poore and couardly, wherfor it would be longe to handel eury seuerall countenance, I leaue it therfore, althoug I could, but tuching or pleassing comly grace I haue sayd somwhat, becausse a sad and heauy countenance (f.4*v*.) in picture is sine of some eiuel, I leaue all the rest to the drawer, to noet by the same example, and let him Read *Lamatzo*, his second bouck of actions and Ieastures wher he shall find good obseruations / wisdome comphrehendeth all things it entereth into all arts, it goeth through them, and considereth of them, it turneth back againe and deuideth them, it placeth them in order and third part, and greatest of all, is the grace in countenance, by which the affections appear, which can neither be well used nor well judged of, but of the wiser sort; and this principal part of the beauty a good painter hath skill of and should diligently note. Wherefore it behoveth him that he be in heart wise, as it will hardly fail that he shall be amorous – and therefore fittest for gentlemen; for who seeth an excellent precious stone, or discerneth an excellent piece of music with skill indeed, and is not moved above others with a more amorous joy and contentment than the vulgar? Howbeit, gentle or vulgar, we are all generally commanded to turn away our eyes from beauty of human shape, lest it inflame the mind. How then can the curious drawer watch, and as it were catch those lovely graces, witty smilings, and those stolen glances which suddenly like lightning pass, and another countenance taketh place, except to behold and very well note and conceit to like? So that he can hardly take them truly, and express them well, without an affectionate good judgment, and without blasting his young and simple heart, although in pleasing admiration he be very serious busied, so hard a matter he hath in hand, calling those graces one by one to their due places: noting how in smiling how the eye changeth and narroweth, holding the sight just between the lids as a centre; how the mouth a little extendeth both ends of the line upwards, the cheeks raise themselves to the eyewards, the nostrils play and are more open, the veins in the temple appear more, and the colour by degrees increaseth, the neck commonly erecteth itself, the eyebrows make the straighter arches, and the forehead casteth itself into a plain as it were for peace and love to walk upon.

In like sort, countenances of wrath, of fear, or of sorrow, have their several alterance of the face, and fare according to how the mind is affected; there be many faces, some lovely, some loathsome, some grave and wise, some foolish and wanton, some proud and audacious, some poor and cowardly; wherefore it would be long to handle every several countenance; I leave it therefore, although I could. But touching on pleasing, comely grace I have said somewhat, because a sad and heavy countenance in a picture is sign of some evil. I leave all the rest to the drawer to note by the same example; and let him read Lomazzo his *Second Book: Of Actions and Gestures*, where he shall find good observations.

Wisdom comprehendeth all things, it entereth into all arts, it goeth through them and considereth of them, it turneth back again and divideth them, it placeth them in order and observeth their several graces.[42] So obserueth their seuerall graces, So Chiefly the drawer should obserue the eys in his pictures, making them so like one to an other, as nature doeth, giuing life to his worke, for the eye is the life of the picture, and be sure likewisse that the sircel of the sight be perfect round, (for so much therof as appeareth) the senter truly placed in the midest therof, the reflection of the light which apeareth like a whit spek, must be placed according to the light, this seemeth but a slight thing, howbeit the most fayleth therin and noet this as the position is, or the drawer placed acording to art, the furthest eye *Position* from the drawer must be a littel higer then the hethermost becausse of the perspectiue if the drawer sit any deall higer then the party drawne, but if lower, then the further eye must be a littel lower, if *life fauor and Liknes* leauel then to be of one hight, so shall the worke by weel placing and trure doing of the eye haue great life, for of all the features in the face of a picture, the eye showeth most life, the nosse the most fauor, and the mouth the most liknes, although liknes is contained in euery part, euen in eury feature, and in the cheekes, chinne, and forhead, with the compasse of the face, but yet cheefly in the mouth, wherfor as I haue formerly sayd that the goodnes or ilnes of the liuing face consisteth in three things

1	*Complection*	
2	*Proportion*	*Being the fauore*
3	*Countenane*	

So remember the goodnes of a picture after the liffe, standeth cheefly also vppon three points

1	*Liffe*		*Eye*
2	*fauor*	wch chiefly consist in thesse three features	*nose*
3	*Liknes*		*mouth.*

fauor and liknes are both one in some sence, as one would say of a picture after the liffe, that it hath the very fauore of the party or the very liknes of the party, both is one thinge, but when one sayeth it is a welfauored picture, and a well like picture, theese differ, so meane I that the nosse giueth cheefe fauor, for one shall neuer see an Ill fauored face, that hath a weel propotioned nosse I find also that many drawers after the life for want of true Ruell or Iugment oftentimes fayles more in true proportion, theen they that without patterne drawe out of thier owne head, euen through the ill setting of the party drawne, which is also (f.5*r*.) the drauers fault, that marketh not when the party remoueth, though it be neuer so littele, for if he one a sudaine remoue a great dealle, then yo marke it chiefly the drawer should observe the eyes in his pictures, making them so like one to another as nature doth, giving life to his work, for the eye is the life of the picture; and be sure likewise that the circle of the sight be perfect round (or so much thereof as appeareth), the centre truly placed in the midst thereof. The reflection of the light, which appeareth like a white speck, must be placed according to the light. This seemeth but a slight thing, howbeit the most faileth therein; and note this: as the position is, or the drawer placed according to art, the furthest eye from the drawer must be a little higher than the hithermost, because of the perspective, if the drawer sit any deal higher than the party drawn; but if lower, then the further eye must be a little lower; if level, then to be of one height. So shall the work by well placing and true doing of the eye have great life; for of all the features in the face of a picture, the eye showeth most life, the nose the most favour, and the mouth the most likeness – although likeness is contained in every part, even in every feature, and in the cheeks, chin and forehead, with the compass of the face; but yet chiefly in the mouth. Wherefore, as I have formerly said that the goodness or illness of the living face consisteth in three things,

Position

Life, favour and likeness

1. Complexion	
2. Proportion	being the favour,
3. Countenance	

so remember the goodness of a picture after the life standeth chiefly also upon three points:

1. Life		Eye
2. Favour	which chiefly consist in	Nose
3. Likeness	these three features	Mouth

Favour and likeness are both one in some sense, as if one would say of a picture after the life that it hath the very favour of the party or the very likeness of the party, both is one thing; but when one sayeth it is a well-favoured picture, and a well-like picture, these differ. So mean I that the nose giveth chief favour, for one shall never see an ill-favoured face that hath a well-proportioned nose.

I find also that many drawers after the life, for want of true rule of judgment, oftentimes fail more in true proportion than they that without pattern draw out of their own head, even through the ill-setting of the party drawn; which is also the drawer's fault that marketh not when the party removeth, though it be never so little. For if he on a sudden remove a great deal, then you mark it easily, and recall him to his first line; but easely, and recall him to his first lyne, but the littele mouing, leadeth yo to a great error, if yo perceiue it not quickly, soe that they somtime make the eyes at one position or standing, the nosse at ane other, the mouth at an other, the eare at an other, I amonish yo of that *Obseruation* fault both Sitter and drawer, wch is the greatest cause of leesinge the liknes in pictures, Marke weel I saye, therfor when yor worke is remoued neuer so littel, recall him to his right waye or place, or proceed not, And to preuent this error, yor marke shalbe yr first line wch yo drawe, but that must be most truly drawne, for that lyne must be a scalle to all the rest / and let that yor first lyne be the +  forehead stroake, as for exampel+ Soe then yo shall proceed by that scalle or scantlinge to doe all proportionablye to that bignes, as × if the forehead be but so longe, then the rest of that lyne to the 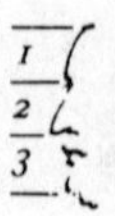 Chine is but twice so long, as thus,× and so proceed still, weel marking when yo loosse that line, that is to say, when that lyne is not to yo, to your seeing, as when yo first sawe it, and drue it for then yr mark is remembred, which yo shall best knowe and perceiue by the distance betwene the eye and that lyne, which also yo must mark howe it was when yo drwee that lyne, howe neare it or howe fare, / *Albert Dure* giueth this rulle / that comonly all faces howld one measure and true proportion (how differing so euer they be of fawor) that the forhead is of the lenght of the nose, and the nose as long as frome the nose to the chinne, if it differ in this it is *Deformety* (by this rule) howebeit I haue knowne to howld in Right good fauors in some feewe, but if I should for example name any it must be such an on as most neuer kneue, or else it can not well be graunted, Sir Chr: Hatton. therfore I wilbe bould to remember me of one namly *Sr C. H:* some times *lorde Chancellor of England* a man generally knowne and respected of all men amongst the best fauours, and to be one of the goodlyest parsonages of england, yet had he a very low forhead, not answerable to that good proportion of a third part of his face, and one the contrary part, Infinit number of face ther are which howld that proportion, which *Albert Duer* commendeth, and yet ar but Il fauored, or vnpleasant faces to behowld (so god in nature hath for diference ordained it) but very rarly doth nature or hardly can *Art* make a good fauor that shall not howld that true proportion / wherfor he was a rare man, and had as Rare fortune which differed therin, for if any of the three it may (f.5*v*.) differ without disgrace to fauore, the forhead maye differ Rather in lenght, and may be the longst, and *Proportion* hinder no fauour, which comonly is seene in the most wisse and the little moving leadeth you to a great error if you perceive it not quickly, so that they sometimes make the eyes at one position or standing, the nose at another, the mouth at another, the ear at another. I admonish you of that fault, both sitter and drawer, which is the greatest cause of losing the likeness in pictures. Mark well, I say therefore, when your work is removed never so little, recall him to his right way or place, or proceed not. *Observation* And to prevent this error, your mark shall be your first line which you draw; but that must be truly drawn, for that line must be a scale to all the rest; and let your first line be the forehead stroke, as for example+ So then you shall proceed by that scale or scantling[43] to do all proportionably to that bigness; as, if the forehead be but so long, then the rest of that line to the chin is but twice so long, as thus×; and so proceed still, well marking when you lose that line, that is to say when that line is not to your seeing as when you first saw it and drew it; for then your mark is remembered; which you shall best know and perceive by the distance between the eye and that line, which also you must mark how it was when you drew that line, how near it or how far.

\+ 

×

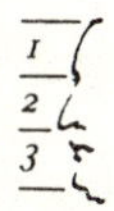

Albert Dürer giveth this rule, that commonly all faces hold one measure and true proportion, how differing soever they be of favour; that the forehead is of the length of the nose, and the nose as long as from the nose to the chin; if it differ in this, it is deformity by this rule. Howbeit, I have known it not[44] to hold in right good favours in some few; but if I should for example name any, it must be such a one as most men knew, or else it cannot well be granted. Therefore I will be bold to remember me of one, namely Sir Christopher Hatton,[45] sometime Lord Chancellor of England, a man generally known and respected of all men amongst the best favours, and held to be one of the goodliest personages of England: yet had he a very low forehead, not answerable to that good proportion of a third part of his face; and on the contrary part, infinite number of faces there are which hold that proportion which Albert Dürer commendeth, and yet are but ill-favoured or unpleasant faces to behold, so God in nature hath for difference ordained it; but very rarely doth nature, nor hardly can art, make a good favour that shall not hold that true proportion. Wherefore he was a rare man, and had as rare fortune, which differed therein; for if any of the three may differ without disgrace to favour, the forehead may differ rather in length, and may be the longest and hinder no favour; which commonly is seen in the most wise and noble-minded *Proportion*

noble minded one and ancient folke, wher the forhead euer waxeth higher and higher, and also doeth the nose (to keepe euen with it) growe a litel longher, or at the least decline at the toppe, but the lower part shortneth, all men see a maruelious change in the face of mankind frome a child to an owld mane, but fewe can tell howe in parts it is wrought so to change by the efect of time first therfore yo shall vnderstand that a child of three years owld hath an eye as bige as a man, at the least the sircle of the sight if not the ball, the nose of no lenght answerable either to the forhead, or distance from the nose downe wards, Ergo *Alberts* porprotion howldeth not in childeren (wherof I knowe he was not ignorant) neither howldeth it in owld folke, for the forhead waxeth higher, the nose longer, and so consequently the mouthe, and chine, somtime for want of teethe shorter, as in men shauen most easaly is deserned, more then in other becausse of theire beards, then *Albert* meant that such proprotion howldeth but at rippe years, as frome fourteene to forty or fiuty, or therabouts / I would willingly giue many obseruations tuching proportion fit to be knowne, but the bouck is great already, wherfor I omit them porposly, yet one wourd more in remembrance Sir P Sidney of an excelent man namly *Sr Philip Sidny*, that noble and most valiant knight that great scoller, and excelent *Poet*, great louer of all vertu and cuninge, he once Demanded of me the question, whether it weare possibl in one scantling, as in the lenght of six inches of a littel or short man, and also of a mighty bige and taulle man in the same scantling, and that one might weel and apparently see which was the taule man, and which the littel, the picture being Iust of one lenght, I showed him that it was easely decerned if it weare cuningly drawne with true obseruations, for ower eye is cuninge, and is learned without rulle by long vsse, as littel lads speake their vulger tonge without gramour Rulls, but I gaue him rules and suficient reasons to noet and obserue, as that the littel man comonly as great as the tawle man, then of nececity the rest of the body must be the lesse in that same scantling, a littel man comonly hath also comonly short legs, and thieghs in comporison to his bulke of body or head, but though the head be as great as the (f.6*r.*) tall mans, yet shall his forme and face and countenace be fare otherwise, easey enough to diserne, the talle man hath comonly low showlders, long shankes, thiegs, armes hands and feet wherwith ouer eye is so comonly aquainted that without rule to vs knowne, it knoweth it straight, but if an ile painter come which will make a childs head as ones, and in ancient folk, where the forehead ever waxeth higher and higher, and also doth the nose, to keep even with it, grow a little longer, or at least decline at the top; but the lower part shortneth.

All men see a marvellous change in the face of mankind from a child to an old man, but few can tell how in parts it is wrought so to change by the effect of time. First therefore, you shall understand that a child of three years old hath an eye as big as a man's, at the least the circle of the sight, if not the ball; the nose of no length answerable either to the forehead or distance from the nose downwards. Ergo Albert's proportion holdeth not in children (wherof I know he was not ignorant); neither holdeth it in old folk, for the forehead waxeth higher, the nose longer, and so consequently the mouth and chin, sometimes for want of teeth, shorter, as in men shaven most easily is discerned, more than in others because of their beards. Then Albert meant that such proportion holdeth but at ripe years, as from fourteen to forty or fifty, or thereabouts.

I would willingly give many observations touching proportion fit to be known, but the book is great already; wherefore I omit them purposely. Yet one word more, in remembrance of an excellent man, namely Sir Philip Sidney, that noble and most valiant knight, that great scholar and excellent poet, great lover of all virtue and cunning. He once demanded of me the question, whether it were possible in one scantling, as in the length of six inches, to have the picture of a little or short man, and also of a mighty, big and tall man in the same scantling, and that one might well and apparently see which was the tall man and which the little, the pictures being just of one length.[46] I showed him that it was easily discerned if it were cunningly drawn with true observations, for our eye is cunning, and is learned without rule by long use, as little lads speak their vulgar tongue without grammar rules. But I gave him rules, and sufficient reasons to note and observe: as that the little man's head being commonly as great as the tall man's, then of necessity the rest of the body must be the less in that same scantling. A little man commonly hath also short legs and thighs in comparison to his bulk of body or head; but though the head be as great as the tall man's, yet shall his form and face and countenance be far otherwise, easy enough to discern. The tall man hath commonly low shoulders, long shanks, thighs, arms, hands and feet, wherewith our eye is so commonly acquainted that without rule to us known it knoweth it straight. But if an ill painter come which will make a child's littel for his body as a tall mans a childe is but fower times the lenght of his face, and a mans tene tymes and more, or his eye as littel for his face as a mans, or his nose as great, I will not take vpon me to knowe his tall man from a dwarfe, there is notwith standinge much faire worke wherin such grosse error is, and much disproportion and false perspectiue / but neatnes and well coulloring worke oft times soe graceth the matter, that common eys neuer note it, but men do beleeue it to be exquesit and perfect becausse of the neatnes, but knowe it yo for a truth, that the cheefest mastery and skill consisteth in the true proportion and line, and a tall mans picture exactly drawne but in the lenght of sixe Inches, shall shewe to be a taller mans picture, then a littel mans picture drawne at the lenght of fowre and twenty inches, or in his owne full height, if his true shape be obserued, and so of horsses and other beasts and cattell the like, *Lamatzo* confirmeth this, by naming some man to be sixe heads, some of tenne, some of twelue, other authors the like, forget not therfore that the principal pte of painting or drawing after the life, consisteh in the truth of the lyne, as one sayeth in a place, that he hath seene the picture of her matie in fower lynes very like, meaning by fower lynes but the playne lynes, as he might as well haue sayd in one lyne, but best in plaine lines without shadowing, for the lyne wthout shadowe showeth all to a good Iugment, but the shadowe without lyne showeth nothing, as fo exampel, though the shadowe of a man against a whit wall showeth like a man, yet is it not the shadowe, but the lyne of the shadowe, which is so true, that it resembleth excelently well, as drawe but that lyne about the shadowe with a coall, and when the shadowe is gone it will resembel better then before, and may if it be a faire face, haue sweet countenance euen in the lyne, for the line only giueth the countenance, but both lyne and coulor giueth the liuely liknes, and shadows showe the roundnes, and the effect or defect of the light wherin the picture was drawne / this makes me to remember the wourds also (f.6*v.*) and reasoning of her matie, when first I came in her highnes presence to drawe, whoe after showing me howe shee notied great difference of shadowing in the works, and diuersity of Drawers of sundry nations, and that the Italians had the name to be cunningest, and to drawe best, shadowed not, Requiring of me the reason of it, seeing that best to showe ones selfe, nedeth no shadow of place but rather the oppen light / to which I graunted, afirmed that shadowes in picturs weare indeed caused by the shadow of the place, or coming in of

Q. Elizabeth

head as little for his body as a tall man's (a child is but four times the length of his face, and a man ten times and more), or his eye as little for his face as a man's, or his nose as great, I will not take upon me to know his tall man from a dwarf. There is notwithstanding, much fair work wherein such gross error is, and much disproportion and false perspective: but neatness and well-colouring the work oft times so grace the matter that common eyes never note it, but men do believe it to be exquisite and perfect because of the neatness. But know it you for a truth that the chiefest mastery and skill consisteth in the true proportion and line, and a tall man's picture exactly drawn but in the length of six inches shall show to be a taller man's picture than a little man's picture drawn at the length of four-and-twenty inches, or in his own full height, if his true shape be observed; and so of horses and other beasts, and cattle the like. Lomazzo confirmeth this by naming some men to be six heads, some of ten, some of twelve: other authors the like.

Forget not therefore that the principal part of painting or drawing after the life consisteth in the truth of the line; as, one sayeth in a place that he hath seen the picture of Her Majesty in four lines very like:[47] meaning by four lines but the plain lines, as he might as well have said in one line. But best in plain lines without shadowing; for the line without shadow showeth all to a good judgment, but the shadow without line showeth nothing: as for example, though the shadow of a man against a white wall showeth like a man, yet it is not the shadow, but the line of the shadow which is so true that it resembleth excellently well; as draw but that line about the shadow with a coal,[48] and when the shadow is gone it will resemble better than before, and may, if it be a fair face, have sweet countenance even in the line, for the line only giveth the countenance; but both line and colour give the lively likeness; and shadows show the roundness, and the effect or defect of the light wherein the picture was drawn.

This makes me to remember the words also and reasoning of Her Majesty when first I came in her Highness's presence to draw; who, after showing me how she noted great difference of shadowing in the works, and the diversity of drawers of sundry nations, and that the Italians, who had the name to be cunningest and to draw best, shadowed not, required of me the reason of it, seeing that best to show oneself needeth no shadow of place, but rather the open light. The which I granted, and affirmed that shadows in pictures were indeed caused by the shadow of the place, the light as only one waye into the place at some small or high windowe which many workmen couet to worke in for ease to their sight, and to giue vnto them a grosser lyne, and a more aparant lyne to be deserned, and maketh the worke inborse well, and shewe very wel afar of, which to *Limning* work nedeth not, because it is to be weewed of nesesity in hand neare vnto the eye, heer her Matie conseued the reason, and therfor chosse her place to sit in for that porposse in the open ally of a goodly garden, where no tree was neere, nor anye shadowe at all, saue that as the heauen is lighter then the earth, soe must that littel shadowe that was from the earthe, this her Matie curiose dmaund hath greatly bettered my Iugment besids diuers other like questions in *Art* by her most excelent Matie which to speake or writ of, weare fitter for some better clarke, *Light* this matter only of the light, let me perfect, that noe wisse man longer remaine in error of praysing much shadowes in pictures after the life, especially small pictures which ar to be wiued in hand, great pictures placed high ore farr of, Requier hard shadowes, or become the better then nearer in story worke better then pictures of the life, for beauty and good fauor is like cleare truth, which is not shamed with the light, nor neede to bee obscured, so a picture a littel shadowed maye be bourne withall for the rounding of it, but so greatly smutted or darkned, as some vsse disgrace it, and is like truth ill towld, if a very weel fauored woman stan in place wher is great shadowe, yet showeth shee louly, not because of the shadow, but becausse of her sweet fauor consisting in the lyne or proportion, euen that littel which the light scarsly sheeweth, greatly pleaseth, mouing the desier to see more, *Ergo* more would see more but if she be not very fayre together with her good proportion (f.7*r*.) As if to palle, too red, or frekled &ce, then shadowe to shewe her in, doeth her a fauore, wherfore I conclud great shadowe is a good signe in a pictur after the life of an ill cause and sheweth plainly that either the drawer had no good sight to diserne his shadowes, except they weare grosse, or had a bad light to drawe in, to high or to lowe, or to littel, or else the party drawne needeth and choose thosse shadowes for the causes aboue sayd, or it was perhaps for some speciall deuice or affection of the stander to be drawne in so standing, knowe this also that to shadowe (sweetly as wee weell calle it) and round well, is a fare greater cuning then shadowing hard or dark, for to round a worke well canot be without some shadowe, but so to shadowe as if it weare not at all shadowed, is best shadowed, for or coming in of the light only one way into the place at some small or high window, which many workmen covet to work in for ease to their sight, and to give unto them a grosser line, and a more apparent line to be discerned; and maketh the work emboss well,[49] and show very well afar off, which to limning work needeth not, because it is to be viewed of necessity in hand near unto the eye. Here Her Majesty conceived the reason, and therefore chose her place to sit in for that purpose in the open alley of a goodly garden, where no tree was near, nor any shadow at all, save that as the heaven is lighter than the earth, so must there be that little shadow that was from the earth. This Her Majesty's curious demand hath greatly bettered my judgment, besides divers other like questions in art by her most excellent Majesty, which to speak or write of were fitter for some better clerk.

This matter only of the light let me perfect, that no wise man longer remain in error of praising much shadows in pictures after the life, especially small pictures which are to be viewed in hand; great pictures placed high or far off require hard shadows, which become them better than nearer; in story work better than pictures of the life. For beauty and good favour is like clear truth, which is not shamed with the light, nor needs to be obscured; so a picture a little shadowed may be borne withal for the rounding of it; but so greatly smutted or darkened as some use, disgraceth it, and is like truth ill told. If a very well favoured woman stand in a place where is great shadow, yet showeth she lovely; not because of the shadow, but because of her sweet favour, consisting in the line or proportion. Even that little which the light scarcely showeth greatly pleaseth, moving the desire to see more, *ergo* more would see more; but if she be not very fair together with her good proportion, as if too pale, too red, or freckled etc., then shadow to show her in doeth her a favour. Wherefore I conclude great shadow is a good sign, in a picture after the life, of an ill cause, and showeth plainly that either the drawer had no good sight to discern his shadows except they were gross, or had a bad light to draw in, too high or too low or too little; or else the party drawn needeth and chose those shadows for the cause above said; or it was perhaps for some special device or affection[50] of the stander to be drawn in so standing. *Light*

Know this also, that to shadow sweetly, as we well call it, and to round well, is a far greater cunning than shadowing hard or dark; for to round a work well cannot be without some shadow; but so to shadow as if it were not at all shadowed is best shadowed, for a round ball is a round a round ball is a round ball in the oppen light, where the light cometh euery way, as weel as in a seller, wher it cometh in at a littel gratt, but euery thing in his true kind is to be allowed of, as is required of necesity in the story or deuice, that is wher the matter consisteth more in a strange light, then in the liknes of the party so drawne, as if one must be drawne or painted blowing the coalle in the darke to light a candel, wee must then shadowe accordingly, making no light, but that which comes from the coale vntill the candel be lighted, so when the action in the story or the deuice in the picture requireth it, them I highly comend it and discomend theire obsurdyty which omit it, as if one should make the troupe of *Iudas* going to seeke *christ* in the garden by night with torches and lanthornes or any fier works, or asaultinge a city by night, and should make a cleare sky and faire day both one them and all the landship, weare it neuer so well painted, it weare not to the purposse or matter, but rediccalious and false, for ther the matter consisteth, consisteth chifly one the trayterous act Done by night and such prouision, as they had for light, more then in any liknes of the lyfe in any of theire pictures / wherfor hee gaue them a signe, saying whome I Kisse, that is he, least they should not see, if hee had but pointed at him, or discribed him, *Paulo Lamatzo* maintaineth mine oppinion more then any other (that euer I hard) in his bouck, saing what is shadowe, *Coullers* but the defect of light / nowe a word or toe (f.7*v*.) of *Coullors*, for which as fit for limning, and which ar not / all ill smelling coullers all ill tasting as *Orpament*, *verdigres*, *verditer*, *Pinck*, *Sapgrene*, *Litmonsy*, or any vnsweet coulers ar naught for *Limning*, vsse none of them if yo may chusse, if *Masticot*, *Ceder grene*, *galleston*, *powncky*, *greene*, *Indy Blewe*, and *vltermarine*, may be gotten, theese and most other cullers ought to be grinded (except the *Litmouse* or *Pansy greene*, which is a sape greene) but wash it first, the finest frome the coursest drosse, and then softly grind it againe, weel cleansing yo stone to euery seuerall collore, nowe to speake of the number of cullers, some authors, sayeth, ther are but toe cullers, which are black and whit, because indeed in whit and black all things are or maye be in a maner very well Discribed, as apeareth in the well grauen portraiture of *Albert Dure*, *Hendrick Goltzius*, and others, and indeed all painting is performed by lighning and shadowing which may be termed whit and black, for light and darknes, in what coullor soeuer it be / therfor first I will speake of whit and black, whether thy be the only coullours, or no coullers at all (as many ball in the open light, where the light cometh every way, as well as in a cellar where it cometh in at a little grate. But everything in his true kind is to be allowed of, as is required of necessity in the story or device: that is, where the matter consisteth more in a strange light than in the likeness of the party so drawn, as if one must be drawn or painted blowing the coal in the dark to light a candle, we must then shadow accordingly, making no light but that which comes from the coal until the candle be lighted. So when the action in the story or the device in the picture requireth it, then I highly commend it, and discommend their absurdity which omit it. As if one should make the troop of Judas going to seek Christ in the garden by night with torches and lanterns, or any fireworks, or assaulting a city by night, and should make a clear sky and fair day, both on them and all the landscape; were it never so well painted, it were not to the purpose or matter, but ridiculous and false; for there the matter consisteth chiefly in the traitorous act done by night, and such provision as they had for light, more than any likeness of the life in any of their pictures. Wherefore he gave them a sign, saying 'Whom I kiss, that is He,' lest they should not see, if he had but pointed at Him or described Him. Paolo Lomazzo maintaineth my opinion more than any other that ever I heard, in his book, saying 'What is shadow but the defect of light?'[51]

Now a word or two of colours,[52] for which are fit for limning and which are not. All ill-smelling colours, all ill-tasting, as orpiment, verdigris, verditer, pink, sap-green, litmus, or any unsweet colours are naught for limning; use none of them if you may choose. If massicot, ceder green, gall-stone, pansy green, indigo and ultramarine may be got, these and most other colours ought to be ground (except the litmus or pansy green, which is a sap-green); but wash it first, the finest from the coarsest dross, and then softly grind it again, well cleansing your stone to every several colour. *Colours*

Now to speak of the number of colours:[53] some authors say there are but two colours, which are black and white, because indeed in white and black all things are, or may be, in a manner very well described, as appeareth in the well engraven portraiture of Albert Durer, Hendrick Goltzius and others; and indeed all painting is performed by lightening and shadowing, which may be termed white and black, for light and darkness, in what colour soever it be. Therefore first I will speak of white and black, whether they be the only colours, or no colours at all, as many

others say) for my part I thinke them worthiest to be first placed *Whits* being the most vssed / of *whits*, *Whitlead* the best pict out and grinded, and dried one a chalke stone in trenches made in the stone for that purpose, and afterwards grinded againe, after a dayes grinding with *Gume Arabeck*, and wash it, it becometh a good *whit* for *limning*, and by the washing to sorts ar mad, Iter *Serusa*, which is made fine, vssed in the same sort and in the making yo shall make
1 three sorts therof / the first and finest, which will glisten, I call
2 sattin whit / the next in finnes is good for *linning* &ce / the last and
2 coursest being once againe grinded, is best to be vssed for the flesh couller properly called cornations, which in no sort ought to haue any glistning / that with a very littel Red lead only aded maketh the fairest carnations, if the party be a littel paller, lesse Read lead and a littel masticot amonge, if yet browner, more of each and a littel oker De Ruse withall / other whits may be made of diuers things as of the bones of a Lambe, and of yong burnt, also of some (f.8*r.*) sheels, as ege shells, and oyster sheels, but thosse whits are to be vssed for other porposses, fitter then for *limning* / ther is also an excelent whit to be made of quicksiluer / which draweth a very fine lyne / this whit the women painters vsse / noet also the sattine seruce grinded with oyle of whit popy, whitneth vpp pearles in oyle coullors most excelently, and it serueth not as the linseed oyle doeth, but it is long in dryinge, this is an experience of mine owne finding *Blackes* out / The best blacke is veluet blacke, wch is *Iuory* burnt in a Crucible and luted that Ayre enter not, mix therfor yr lutting with a littel salt, and let it nealle redd hot a quarter of an hower, then lett it coole, and grind it with *Gume watter* only, and washe it, in this maner, power watter to it by littel and littel, still stirringe it, and when it is as thine as Inke or thinner, let yt settele a wholle afternoone, and poure from it the vppermost, wch is but the Gume and fowlnes, good to put amonge Inke, the rest let drye, and keepe it in a paper or boxe, and vsse it as aforsaid, wth soft grinding it againe, or tempering, but one the grinding stone wth watter adding Gume in powder to it againe at discretion, ffor yo shall by vssing it, perceive if it haue too littel gume, for then it worketh ill, and dryeth to fast, if yo put too much gume, then it wilbe some what bright lyke oyle callor, wch is vylde in *lymning* / Take this for a generall rule, that *Lymning* must excell all *Painting* in that point, in that it must giue eury thing his proper lustre as weel as his true cullor light and shadowe. / Other blackes are made in lyke maner, as of

others say. For my part, I think them worthiest to be first placed, being the most used.

Whites Of whites, white lead is the best, picked out and grinded, and dried on a chalk stone in trenches made in the stone for that purpose, and afterwards grinded again; after a day's grinding with gum arabic and washing, it becometh a good white for limning, and by the washing two sorts are made. *Item*[54] ceruse, which made fine, used in the same sort; and in the
making you shall make three sorts thereof:[55] the first and finest, which *1*
will glisten, I call satin white; the next in fineness is good for limning etc.; *2*
the last and coarsest, being once again grinded, is best to be used for the *3*
flesh colour, properly called carnation, which in no sort ought to have any glistening. That, with a very little red lead only added, maketh the fairest carnations; if the party be a little paler, less red lead and a little massicot among; if yet browner, more of each and a little ochre de rouse withal. Other whites may be made of divers things, as of the bones of a lamb and of a young pig[56] burnt, also of some shells, as egg shells and oyster shells; but those whites are to be used for other purposes fitter than for limning. There is also an excellent white to be made of quicksilver which draweth a very fine line; this white the women painters use.[57] Note also the satin ceruse grinded with oil of white poppy whiteneth up pearls in oil colours most excellently; and it serveth not as the linseed oil doth, but it is long in drying. This is an experience of mine own finding out.

Blacks The best black is velvet black, which is ivory burnt in a crucible, and luted,[58] that air enter not; mix therefore your luting with a little salt; and let it anneal[59] red hot a quarter of an hour, then let it cool and grind it with gum water only, and wash it in this manner: pour water to it by little and little, still stirring it, and when it is as thin as ink, or thinner, let it settle a whole afternoon, and pour from it the uppermost, which is but the gum and foulness, good to put among ink. The rest let dry, and keep it in a paper or box and use it as aforesaid with soft grinding of it again, or tempering, but on the grinding stone with water adding gum in powder to it again at discretion; for you shall by using it perceive if it have too little gum, for then it workest ill and dryeth too fast; if you put too much gum then it will be somewhat bright, like oil colour, which is vile in limning. Take this for a general rule, that limning must excell all painting in that point, in that it must give everything his proper lustre, as well as his true colour, light and shadow. Other blacks are made in like manner,

Chery stones, *Datestones*, *Peachstones*, and common *Charkecole*, *willowecolle*, or any thinge that burneth burneth blacke, these burnt and grinded as aforesaid, but they need no washinge / Noate also that veluet blacke after it is drye in the Shell, it worketh neuer more soe weell, as at the first grinding or tempering, wherfore for principall workes, and euen for the Centor of the eye, being but a littel tytle, I vse alwayes to temper a lyttle one my grinding stone, hauing it alwayes in powder ready grinded, washt, and dryed for store, Soe vse I to haue most of my other cullors, that I may easely temper then wth my finger in a shell, adding *Gume* at discretion / soe haue I them allwayes cleane and fayer, and easyer to worke. / Thus a limner should doe, but for sparing time and cost, (f.8*v*.) some vsse to worke out of theire ould Shells of cullors, thoughe they be naught and dusty /

His own Practice

Now besides whittes and blacks, there are but fiue other principall cullors, wch are cullors of perfecton in themselues, not participatinge wth any other, nor can be made of any other mixed cullors, and of them fiue, are neuerthelesse dyuers kinds, so as wth them are made by mixture *Murrey*, *Redd*, *Blewe*, *greene*, and *yellow* / .

Murreys *1* first murreye for *Limning* must be a lake of himselfe of a murrey cullore, which kind of Lake is best made at *Venice* and neatly good in *Antwerpen*, If yo be driuen of other lake wth adding a littel blewe to it, to make yr murrey it can neuer be so good. / This lake is to be grinded but wth gume *Arrabecke* watter only, although when it is ouer drye in the shell, yt hardly relenteth to worke weel againe, then grind more. / .

Redds: *2* Redd for *Liming*, the best is lake of *India*, wch breaketh of a Scarlet or stamel cullor, dyuers othe lakes ther are, some wch will shadowe one vppon an other they are so blacke / and all thosse blacke lacks generally must be grinded wth some sugercandye amonge the gume, and some altogether with suger, they cannot be to much grinded nor need any washinge, longe standinge open in the sune marreth yr lakes, and allmost all collors, so ouer baking them, hardninge, or drying them that they will neuer worke well / *vermelion* is an other redd, and is to be grinded and washt, *Redd lead* to be but washt only, the finest of it to *Liminge* twoo sorts of it. /

Blewes *3* for *Limning* the darkest and highest *Blewe* is *Vltermaryne* of *Venice* of the best, I haue payed iijsviijd a Carret wch is but fower graines, xj ll xs the ounce, and the worst which is is but badd will cost ijs vjd the Carret vij ll xs the ounce, In steed wherof wee vse smalt of as of cherry stones, date stones, peach stones, and common charcoal, willowcoal, or anything that burneth black; these burnt and grinded as aforesaid, but they need no washing. Note also that velvet black, after it is dry in the shell, it worketh never more so well as at the first grinding or tempering; wherefore for principal works, and even for the centre of the eye, being but a little tittle, I use always to temper a little on my grinding stone, having it always in powder ready grinded, washed and dryed for store. So use I to have most of my other colours, that I may easily temper them with my finger in a shell, adding gum at discretion; so have I them always clean and fair and easier to work. Thus a limner should do; but for sparing time and cost some use to work out of their old shells of colours, though they be naught and dusty.

Now besides whites and blacks there are but five other principal colours which are colours of perfection in themselves, not participating with any other, nor can be made of any other mixed colours. And of them five are nevertheless divers kinds, which with them are made by mixture: murrey, red, blue, green and yellow.[60]

First, murrey for limning must be a lake of himself of a murrey colour, which kind of lake is best made at Venice, and neatly good in Antwerp. If you be driven to the use of other lake, with adding a little blue to it to make your murrey, it can never be so good. This lake is to be grinded but with gum arabic water only, although when it is over-dry in the shell it hardly relenteth to work well again; then grind more. *1. Murreys*

Red for limning: the best is lake of India, which breaketh of a scarlet or stammel[61] colour. Divers other lakes there are, some which will shadow one upon another, they are so black; and all those black lakes generally must be grinded with some sugar candy among the gum, and some altogether with sugar. They cannot be too much grinded, nor need any washing. Long standing open in the sun marreth your lakes, and almost all colours, so overbaking them, hardening or drying them that they will never work well. Vermilion is another red, and is to be grinded and washed, red lead to be but washed only, the finest of it to limning; two sorts of it. *2. Reds*

For limning, the darkest and highest blue is ultramarine of Venice. Of the best I have paid three shillings and eightpence a carat, which is but four grains – eleven pounds ten shillings the ounce; and the worst, which is but bad, will cost two shillings and sixpence the carat – seven pounds ten shillings the ounce. Instead whereof we use smalt, of the best; blue *3. Blues* the best, blewe byces of diuers sorts, some paler then other, some of seauen or sixe degrees one aboue another / Theise may be grinded, but better broken lyke *Ammel* in a stone morter of flint excelent smouthe, with a pestel of fflint o *Aggat* well stirred till it be fine wth gume watter only, and washed, soe haue yo many sorts, and all good, shadowinge blews are Litmouse and Indy Blewe, and flory, theese need no washing, nor litmouse any grinding, but steeped in lee of sope ashes, vse gume at discretion as aforsaid. /.

Greens Greene the best for *liming* is Ceder greene, Insteed wherof wee
4 take *verditer*, *Pinke* is also a nedfull greene in (f.9*r*.) *Lantscippe*, and mixed with *Byce* ashes makes an other faire deepe greene, so likwise yr pincke mixed with masticot and serusa as yo see cause for light greens / All theese neede washing and not grinding, and all common greens, as common *Sapgreene*, *flower De luce greene*, or pauncy greene neede neither grinding nor washing, but steepinge in watter, or in lee wch is better. / .

Yeallowes *Yeallowe* the best are masticotts, wherof there are duers sorts,
5 some paller then some, yeallowe *Oker* for want of better is one also, and these washt and not grinded doe best, and must haue a littel suger amonge the *Gume* in tempering them / *Shadowing Yeallowes* are the stones found in the oxe gall, grinded with gume watter and not washt, and yeallows made of whit roses brused wth a littel *Allumm* and strayned, and neither grinded not washt, nor nedeth gume, one maye shifte with faire oker de *Rouse*, and safaran watter for want of the other, first shadowe vppon masticote wth yealowe Oker, and with oker de *Rouse*, for shadowinge cullors which are browne, or blackishe, or heire cullor, which are as necesary as any other cullors, yo haue earth of cullen, *Vmber*, *Spalte*, and *oker Rouse*, and *Soote* may also be vssed in story worke, gume watter vse only vnto these. /. a word I praye yo tuchinge the making of those beautifull rubies or other stones, how yo soe arteficially doe them, that being neuer so littel they seme precious *Stones* naturall, cleere and perspicious, soe that (by yr fauor) is no parte of *limming*, / wherfore requier it not, it appertaineth merly to ane other arte / And though I vse it in my limming, it is but as a mayson or Ioyner, when he hath done his worke, and cane also paynt or guilde his freeses and needfull parts therof / Now that yo haue true waye for orderinge yr coullors, vnderstand that in drawing after the life, yo must not
Parchment change yr light, but end yr worke in the same light yo begane in,
or Vellum if yo posibley maye, / knowe also that *Parchment* is the only good

bices of divers sorts, some paler than others, some of seven or six degrees one above another. These may be grinded, but better broken like enamel in a stone mortar of flint excellent smooth, with a pestle of flint or agate, well stirred till it be fine, with gum water only, and washed; so have you many sorts, and all good. Shadowing blues are litmus and indigo, and florey; these need no washing, nor litmus any grinding, but steeped in lye of soap-ashes;[62] use gum at discretion as aforesaid.

Green: the best for limning is ceder green, instead whereof we take verditer. Pink is also a needful green in landscapes, and mixed with bice ashes makes another fair, deep green: so likewise your pink may be mixed with massicot and ceruse as you see cause for light greens. All these need washing and not grinding, and all shadowing[63] greens, as common sap-green, fleur-de-lys green, or pansy-green, need neither grinding nor washing, but steeping in water, or in lye which is better. *4. Greens*

Yellow: the best are massicots, whereof there are divers sorts, some paler than others; yellow ochre, for want of better, is one also; and these washed and not grinded do best, and must have a little sugar amongst the gum in tempering them. Shadowing yellows are the stones found in the ox gall, grinded with gum water and not washed, and yellows made of white roses bruised with a little alum and strained, and neither grinded nor washed, nor needeth gum. One may shift with fair ochre de rouse and saffron water for want of the other; first shadow upon massicot with yellow ochre, and with ochre de rouse. For shadowing colours which are brown or blackish or hair colour, which are as necessary as any other colours, you have earth of Cologne, umber, asphaltum, and ochre de rouse; and soot may also be used in story work; gum water use only unto these. *5. Yellows*

A word, I pray you, touching the making of those beautiful rubies or other stones, how you so artificially do them, that being never so little they seem precious stones, natural, clear and perspicuous; so that (by your favour) is no part of limning, wherefore require it not. It appertaineth merely to another art; and though I use it in my limning, it is but as a mason or joiner, when he hath done his work, and can also paint or gild his friezes and needful parts thereof.

Now that you have true way for ordering your colours, understand that in drawing after the life you must not change your light, but end your work in the same light you begun in, if you possibly may.

Know also that parchment is the only good and best thing to limn on, and best thinge to limme one, but it must be virgine *Parchment*, such as neuer bore haire, but younge things found in the dames bellye./ some calle it *Vellym*, some *Abertiue* deriued frome the word *Abhortiue*, for vntimly birthe, It must be most finly drest, as smothe as any sattine, and pasted with starch well strained one pastbourd well burnished, that it maye be pure without speckes or Staynes, very

Carnations

smoothe and white. /. Then must yo laye yr carnation flowing, and not thine driuen as ane oyle cullore, and when yo begine yr picture choose yr carnations too fayre, for in working yo may make (f.9*v*.) it as browne as yo will, but being chosen to browne, yo shall neuer worke it fayer enough. / for *Limming* is but a shadowing of the same cullor yor grownd is of, and soe generally all ground cullor in limming Must be layd flowing, not toe full flowing, neither for cockling yr carde &c. but some what flowing that it dry not befor yr Pensill, vntill yo haue done, least it seeme patched and roughe / also when you drawe vppon the said complection a Carnation ground culler, be verye well aduised what lines yo drawe, and drawe them very lightly with some of the same carnation and a littel lake amonge very thinly mixtwned, or with thine lake alone wth a very smalle pensile, that it scarce at first maye be discerned, till yo be sure yo bee in the right waye, for afterwards ther is no alteration when the lyne is apparant, or very hardly. / Therfore in yr shadowing vsse also the same discretion to shadowe, but by littel and littel at the first, for littel not regarding what the ignorant say, wch wilbe alwayes teaching, for there be faults which must be done of porposse, being faults which may be amended, for feare yo comit faults which cannot be amended. / ffor the face made neuer so littel to redd, or to browne in limning is neuer to be amended, the face to leane, the forehead to lowe, or haire to darke, is not, or very hardly to be amended, but the botching or mending wilbe perceiued wher one hath taken away any caler one the face, for the carnation will neuer be of the same cullor againe, nor will Ioyne so smoothe, wher any other cullor hath bene layde. /. make the forheade to highe at the first, therfore to be sure yo maye mend it, and be not hastye to lessen it at euery mans worde, but proceede wth Iugment, / I haue euer noted that the better and wiser sort will haue a great patience, and marke the proceedinges of the workman, and neuer find fault till

Criticisms of his sitters

albe fynished, If they find a fault, they doe but saye, I thinke it is to much thus or thus, referring it to better Iugment, but the Ignoranter and basser sort, will not only be bould precisly to say, but

but it must be virgin parchment, such as never bore hair, but young things found in the dam's belly. Some call it vellum, some abertive, derived from the word abortive for untimely birth. It must be most finely dressed, as smooth as any satin, and pasted, with starch well strained, on pasteboard well burnished, that it may be pure, without specks or stains, very smooth and white.

Carnations

Then must you lay your carnation flowing, and not thin driven as an oil colour; and when you begin your picture, choose your carnations too fair, for in working you may make it as brown as you will, but being chosen too brown you shall never work it fair enough. For limning is but a shadowing of the same colour your ground is of, and so generally all ground colour in limning must be laid flowing, not too full flowing neither, for cockling your card etc., but somewhat flowing, that it dry not before your pencil until you have done, lest it seem patched and rough. Also when you draw upon the said complexion of carnation ground colour, be very well advised what lines you draw, and draw them very lightly with some of the same carnation and a little lake among, very thinly mixed, or with thin lake alone, with a very small pencil, that it scarce at first may be discerned, till you be sure you be in the right way; for afterwards there is no alteration when the line is apparent, or very hardly. Therefore in your shadowing use also the same discretion, to shadow but by little and little at the first; for little is best, not regarding what the ignorant say, which will be always teaching. For there be faults which must be done of purpose, being faults which may be amended, for fear you commit faults which cannot be amended; for the face made never so little too red or too brown in limning is never to be amended; the face too lean, the forehead too low, or hair too dark, is not, or very hardly, to be amended. But the botching or mending will be perceived where one hath taken away any colour on the face, for the carnation will never be of the same colour again, nor will join so smooth where any other colour hath been laid. Make the forehead too high at the first, therefore, to be sure you may mend it; and be not hasty to lessen it at every man's word, but proceed with judgment.

I have ever noted that the better and wiser sort will have a great patience, and mark the proceedings of the workman, and never find fault till all be finished. If they find a fault they do but say 'I think it is too much thus, or thus,' referring it to better judgment; but the ignoranter and baser sort will not only be bold precisely to say, but vehemently swear that it vemently sweare that it is thus or soe, and sweare soe contrarely, that this volume would not containe the rediculious absurd speeches wch I have hard vppon such occasions, Theis teachers and bould speakers are commonly seruants of rude vnderstandinge, wch partly would flater, and partly shewe but howe bowld they may be to speake thire opinions, / my Counsel is that a mane should not be moued to anger for the matter, but proceede with his worke in order, and pittie thyer Ignorance (f. 10*r*.), being sure they will neuer robe men of their cuning, but of their worke peraduenture if they can / for commonly wher the Witte is small, the consience is lesse, when yor cullors are drye in the shell, yo are to temper them wth yor ringe finger very cleane when yo will vsse therof, adding a littel gume if it temper not well and flowingly, but beware of to much, if any cullor crack to much in the shell, temper therwth a littele sugar candye, but a very littel least it make it shine, want of guming it causeth the cullor tempere like *Lome* or *Claye* &c and drawes no fine line, if a cullor will not take by Reason that some sweatye hand hand or fattye finger hath touched yor parchment therabout, temper with that cullor a very littel eare waxe, but euen to giue it but a tast as it weare, the same is good likewyse if any cullor pill of to temper the Cullor you amend it with all, and it will pill no more. / liqued goolde and Silluer must not be tempered with the finger, but only wth the penssel, and wth as littel gume as will but bind it that it wype not of with euery touch, and with a prety littel toothe of some fferret or Stoat, or other willde littele beast, / yo maye burnish yr goold or siluer here or there as neede requireth, as yr siluer when yo make yr *Diamonds* first burnished / then drawne vppon with black in Squares lyke the diamond cutt, other stones must be glased vppon the Siluer wth their proper cullors wth some varnish &c. /. The pearles layed with a whit mixed wth a littel black, a littel Indy blewe, and a littel masticot, but very littel in comparison of the whit, not the hundred parte. /. That being dry, giue the light of yr *Pearle* wth siluer some what more to the light side then the shadowe side, and as Round and full as yo cane, then take good whit delayed with a littel *Masticot*, and vnderneath at the shadowe side giue it a Compassing stroke wch showes the reflection that a *Pearle* hath then wthout that a smale Shadowe of Seacole vndermost of all. /. *Paulo Lamatius* in the last chapter of his fowerth bouck very truly (but absurd) sheweth that euery thing must be shadowed in his kind, wch discretion is not giuen to euery painter after the liffe, but they

Diamons and Pearle and other Stones

is thus or so, and swear so contrarily that this volume would not contain the ridiculous, absurd speeches which I have heard upon such occasions. These teachers and bold speakers are commonly servants of rude understanding, which partly would flatter, and partly show but how bold they may be to speak their opinions. My counsel is that a man should not be moved to anger for the matter, but proceed with his work in order, and pity their ignorance, being sure they will never rob men of their cunning, but of their work peradventure, if they can; for commonly where the wit is small, the conscience is less.

When your colours are dry in the shell, you are to temper them with your ring finger, very clean when you will use thereof, adding a little gum if it temper not well and flowingly; but beware of too much. If any colour crack too much in the shell, temper therewith a little sugar candy; but a very little, lest it make it shine. Want of gumming it causeth the colour to temper like loam or clay, etc., and draws no fine line. If a colour will not take by reason that some sweaty hand or fatty finger hath touched your parchment thereabout, temper with that colour a very little ear-wax, but even to give it but a taste as it were; the same is good likewise if any colour peel off; to temper the colour you amend it withal, and it will peel no more. Liquid gold and silver must not be tempered with the finger, but only with the pencil, and with as little gum as will but bind it that it wipe not off with every touch. And with a pretty little tooth of some ferret or stoat or other wild little beast you may burnish your gold or silver here or there as need requireth; as your silver, when you make your diamonds, is first burnished, then drawn upon with black in squares like the diamond cut. Other stones must be glazed upon the silver with their proper colours with some varnish etc.; the pearls laid with a white mixed with a little black, a little indigo, and a little massicot, but very little in comparison of the white, not the hundredth part. That being dry, give the light of your pearl with silver, somewhat more to the light side than the shadow side and as round and full as you can; then take good white, delayed[64] with a little massicot, and underneath at the shadow side give it a compassing stroke, which shows the reflection that a pearl hath; then, without that, a small shadow of seacoal undermost of all.[65] Paolo Lomazzo in the last chapter of his fourth book very truly (but absurdly) showeth that everything must be shadowed in his kind;[66] which discretion is not given to every painter after the life; but they will shadow a fair face with

Diamonds and pearl and other stones

will shadowe a faire face wth a browne shadowe, and following the story works which Shadowes the whole face wth one shadowe for *Shadowing* hast. /. Shadowing in *Lymning* must not be driuen with the flat of the pensel as in Oyle worke, (f.10*v*.) distemper or washing, but with the pointe of the *Pencell* by littel light touches wth cullor very thine, and like hatches as wee call it wth the pen, though the shadowe be neuer so great, it must be all so done by littel touches, and touch not to longe in one place, least it glisten, but let it dry ane howre or to, then dipen it againe. / Wherfore hatching wth the pene in Imitation of some fine well grauen portrature of *Albertus Dure* small peeces, is first to be practised and vsed, bfore one begine to *Limme*, and not to learne to limne at all, till one canne Imitate the *Print* so well, as one shall not knowe the one frome the other, that he maye be able to handle the pensill point in like sort, This is the true order and principall Secret in *Limning*, which that it maye be the better remembred, I end with it. /.

And nowe I thinke it fitt also to speake somwhat of precious stones, which wilbe meet for gentelmen to vnderstand, and some gouldsmithes wilbe glad to see it for their better Instruction, I saye for certayne truth, that ther are besides whit, and black but fyue perfect cullors in the world which I proue by the fyue principall precious stones (bearing cullor) and which are all bright and transparent stones, as followeth, Theise are the fyue stones / *Ammatist orient for Murrey*, *Rubie* for red, *Saphire* for blewe, *Emrod* for greene, and hard *Orient Topies* for yellowe, more ther are not wch are soe very hard and orient as these fyue, ./. Nowe is proued, that the absolute Orient & hardest transparent precious stones of proper and vnmixed cullors are only fyue / viz

Annatist	*Murrey*	theese fyue only cullors in grosse cullors, wth theire different mixtures, make more of many kinds, euenen all maner of cullors as you list to haue them, by tempering them together wch weare long to repeate in writing. /.
Rubye	*Redd*	
Saphier	*Blewe*	
Emarod	*Greene*	
Topias orientall	*Yeallowe*	

Rainbowe And as for mxture of cullors, if yo will see fine varyetie, behold the *Rainbowe*, and therin shall yo find an excellent mixture of all the transparent cullors, for there is nothing but mixt cullors./. As first Murrey, by mixture growing into or vnto blewe./. Blewe growing into greene, Greene growing into yellow / yellow into redd, red

a brown shadow, following the story works, which shadow the whole face with one shadow for haste.

Shadowing

Shadowing in limning must not be driven with the flat of the pencil, as in oil work, distemper, or washing,[67] but with the point of the pencil by little light touches, with colour very thin, and like hatches, as we call it, with the pen. Though the shadow be never so great it must be all so done by little touches; and touch not too long in one place, lest it glisten, but let it dry an hour or two, then deepen it again. Wherefore hatching with the pen, in imitation of some fine, well engraven portraiture of Albertus Dürer's small pieces is first to be practised and used before one begins to limn; and not to learn to limn at all till one can imitate the print so well as one shall not know the one from the other, that he may be able to handle the pencil point in like sort. This is the true order and principle secret in limning, which that it may be the better remembered, I end with it.

And now I think it fit also to speak somewhat of precious stones, which will be meet for gentlemen to understand; and some goldsmiths will be glad to see it for their better instruction. I say for certain truth that there are besides white and black but five perfect colours in the world, which I prove by the five principal precious stones bearing colour, and which are all bright and transparent stones, as followeth.[68] These are the five stones: amethyst orient for murrey, ruby for red, sapphire for blue, emerald for green, and hard orient topaz for yellow. More there are not which are so very hard and orient[69] as these five. Now is it proved that the absolute orient and hardest transparent precious stones of proper and unmixed colours are only five, viz:

Amethyst	Murrey	These five only colours, in gross colours, with their different mixtures, make more of many kinds; even all manner of colours as you list to have them, by tempering them together, which were long to repeat in writing.[70]
Ruby	Red	
Sapphire	Blue	
Emerald	Green	
Topaz orient	Yellow	

Rainbow

And as for mixture of colours, if you will see fine variety, behold the rainbow, and therein shall you find an excellent mixture of all the transparent colours, for there is nothing but mixed colours; as, first murrey, by mixture growing into or unto blue, blue growing into green, green growing into yellow, yellow into red, red again into murrey, murrey into againe into murrey, Murrey into a purpel being mixed with the skey cullor, This exampel (f.11*r*.) of the *Rainbowe* sheweth the naturall mixture of cullors, and a sweete and agreeable varietie in their mixtures / for they vary, and agree in such a kindly beautiful order, as all the art of the worlde cannot amend it by mixture or other order, nor well in Arte compare by imitation wth the same. /. But the fyue precious Stones resemble vnto vs the true beautie of each perfect cullor in his full perfection wthout mixture in perfect hard bodies and very transparent./.

Annatist Orient As first of Murrey./. In the *Annatist orient* haue yo only perfect Murrey without mixture, it is an hard Stone, and on of the principall precious Stones, there are diuers more kinds of *Annatists*, as *Annatist Almane*, & *Annatists* of Sundry other countrys, colde Regions, all which are of diuers other cullors./. I would speake only of theese fyue which I haue nominated, but least men should be deceiued or mistaken. I am forced to name and mention the other baser stones of all the cullors, as of *Annatist Almane*, some are purple, some violett, some Carnation, some peach cullor, and some a browne smoakye cullor like watter wherin Soote hath layen, and of all theise cullors their is great variety of each some paller then other, theise are as I sayd before all mixed cullors, and softe Stones in each of the fyue kinds of stones, as I will hereafter sheewe yo./. Take this therfor for a generall Rulle, that the most precious stones the hardest deerest and rarest to fynde, are those fyue only wch I haue named, and wch haue theire proper cullors only in them / and that of more substance and beauty transpareant and pure, not of a thicke or troubled matter, but clere and yet not pale, wherfore as I haue formerly spoken of the *Annatist Orient*, it is a hard stone and right precious, delighting the hart exceedingly the hart exceedingly to behould, but all the other repeated mixt cullors are softe Stones of smale value in comparison to those of perfect cullors, and although a very darke purpule is founde in some of the *Annatist Almaine*, a cullor of a more substance for his cullor, I saye vnto yo as before I haue sayd / Purpole is not a proper cullor, but mixt cullor, made of Murrey & blewe, or redd and blewe, soe ouer blewed and darkened that the french men rightly terme it *Annatist le plus* (f.11*v*.) *triste*, a sade malancholy cullor, delighting but some humore, and fitting to porpose but one some fewe occasions./. Noate also that the *Annatist oryent* being a perfect cullor, and a hard stone, hath therfore his watter more bright and lucide then any soft Stone cane haue / wch a purple, being mixed with the sky colour. This example of the rainbow showeth the natural mixture of colours, and a sweet and agreeable variety in their mixtures; for they vary and agree in such a kindly beautiful order, as all the art of the world cannot amend it by mixture or other order, nor well in art compare by imitation with the same. But the five precious stones resemble unto us the true beauty of each perfect colour in his full perfection, without mixture, in perfect hard bodies and very transparent.

Amethyst orient

As first, of murrey: in the amethyst orient you have your only perfect murrey without mixture; it is a hard stone, and one of the principal precious stones. There are divers more kinds of amethysts, as amethyst almain[71] and amethysts of sundry other countries, cold regions, all of which are of divers other colours. I would speak only of these five which I have nominated, but lest men should be deceived or mistaken I am forced to name and mention the other baser stones of all the colours, as of amethyst almain. Some are purple, some violet, some carnation, some peach colour, and some a brown, smoky colour, like water wherein soot hath lain; and of all these colours there is great variety of each, some paler than others. These are, as I said before, all mixed colours, and soft stones in each of the five kinds of stones, as I will hereafter show you. Take this therefore for a general rule, that the most precious stones, the hardest, dearest, and rarest to find, are those five only which I have named, and which have their proper colours only in them, and that of more substance and beauty, transparent and pure, not of a thick or troubled water,[72] but clear, and yet not pale. Wherefore, as I have formerly spoken of the amethyst orient, it is a hard stone and right precious, delighting the heart exceedingly to behold; but all the other repeated mixed colours are soft stones of small value in comparison to those of perfect colours. And although a very dark purple is found in some of the amethysts almain (a colour of more substance), for his colour, I say unto you, as before I have said, purple is not a proper colour but a mixed colour,[73] made of murrey and blue or red and blue, so over-blued and darkened that the Frenchmen rightly term it amethyst *le plus triste*, a sad melancholy colour, delighting but some humours, and fitting to purpose but on some few occasions. Note also that the amethyst orient, being a perfect colour and a hard stone, hath therefore his water more bright and lucid than any soft stone can brightnes is the cheefe thinge wherby the *Lapidarie* knoweth at the first sight the vallewe, goodnes, and hardnes of the stone, as shalbe more plainely shewed in the diamond hereafter./. Noate therfore when any Stone wanteth that liuely brightnes, it is either a Safte Stone, a thine Stone, or a clowdye faulty Stone, althoughe it be hard./.

Rubye Now the next perfect cullor wch is redd, the *Rubye* is the most perfect redd, and if he be without blemish, and so great and thicke as he maye beare the proportion of *Diamond Cut*, he flickereth and afecteth the eye like burning fyer, especially by the candel light./. This Stone therfore of some is called, and rightly maye be called the carbunckle / soe called the worde *Carbo* wch is fyer, or a cole of fyer, neither is ther any other *Carbunckel* wch cane resemble fyer so well, except a redd *Diamond* wch yet I neuer Sawe, but haue harde of only, yet haue I seene a *Diamond* of the cullor of a *Iasent*, some what orrenge tawny, and a *Diamond* greene as a *Grisolytt*, and a *Diamond* blewe as a pale blew Sapihire / many yellowe, and many browne./. The *Rubye* ballas is more pale lyke a pale wine, and no perfect full cullor, and it is therfore a softer Sone, and of lesse valewe, soe are all *Rubye ballas*, now *Spynells* and *Garnets* of diuers Sorts are reddish also, and resemble rubyes and *Annatists orient* meetelye well / but they are to be knowne by the softnes on the myll in cutting, and partly by theire want of that brightnes, wch the hard Stone hath, and want of perfect cullor, but a redd mixed with yeallowe more fyer then perfect redd, a Stone of much delight, and good valewe, but of less then the *Rubie*, for it is softer, as all mixed cullors are softer then the perfect cullors, and of the *Spinalls* also ther are a paler kinde lyke a delicate ould paled wyne wch resemble *Rubie ballas* in like maner./.

Garnetts Also *Garnets* there are sundry sorts, some called garnets *Suryma*, resembling much the *Annatist orient*, but a littel blacker & redder then the true Murrey./ The more common sorte of garnetts are very redish, yea blacker then true redd, and somewhat yeallowish *Iasent labella* is a kinde of redd, very yeallowish (f.12*r*.) like the *saffreon* blade, but transparent and beautifull as any *Spinaller Garnett*, and as hard and bright, the common Iasent is Orrenge tawnye, a mixt cullor also./.

Vermyle Then ther is an other kind of redd stone called vermyle, wch are very small and neuer found greatter then a pease, but commonly no biger then rapeseed, a red more resembling blood then *Rubye*, and have; which brightness is the chief thing whereby the lapidary knoweth at the first sight the value, goodness, and hardness of the stone, as shall be more plainly showed in the diamond hereafter. Note therefore, when any stone wanteth that lively brightness, it is either a soft stone, a thin stone, or a cloudy, faulty stone, although it be hard.

Now the next perfect colour, which is red: the ruby is the most perfect *Ruby* red, and if he be without blemish, and so great and thick as he may bear the proportion of diamond cut, he flickereth and affecteth the eye like burning fire, especially by the candle light. This stone therefore of some is called, and rightly may be called, the carbuncle, so called from the word *carbo*, which is fire, or a coal of fire; neither is there any other carbuncle which can resemble fire so well, except a red diamond, which yet I never saw, but have heard of only. Yet have I seen a diamond of the colour of a jacinth, somewhat orange tawny, and a diamond green as a chrysolite, and a diamond blue as a pale blue sapphire, many yellow and many brown. The balas ruby[74] is more pale, like a pale wine, and no perfect full colour, and it is therefore a softer stone, and of less value; so are all balas rubies. Now spinels and garnets of divers sorts are reddish also, and resemble rubies and amethysts orient meetly well, but they are to be known by the softness on the mill in cutting, and partly by their want of that brightness which the hard stone hath, and want of perfect colour; but a red mixed with yellow hath more fire than perfect red, a stone of much delight and good value, but of less than the ruby, for it is softer, as all mixed colours are softer than the perfect colours. And of the spinels also there are a paler kind, like a delicate, old pale wine, which resemble balas rubies in like manner.

Also garnets there are of sundry sorts, some called Syriam[75] garnets *Garnets* resembling much the amethyst orient, but a little blacker and redder than the true murrey. The more common sorts of garnet are very reddish, yea blacker than true red, and somewhat yellowish. Jacinth labella is a kind of red, very yellowish, like the saffron blade, but transparent and beautiful as any spinel or garnet, and as hard and bright. The common jacinth is orange tawny, a mixed colour also.

Then there is another kind of red stone called vermeil,[76] which are very *Vermeil* small and never found greater than a pea, but commonly no bigger than rapeseed; a red more resembling blood than ruby, and is not that perfect is not that perfect crimson redd, most like the kirnelles of very ripe *Pomegranat*, wch nature hath commended vnto vs in the *Rubye* to be the principall red cullor, yet this littel poore Stone hath that speciall vertue to endure the fyre, wch none of the for named Stones cann doe Soe well./.

Saphire Blewe Nowe *Saphire* wherof there be two kinds or two cullors, white and blewe, wch blewe is the most excelent perfect blewe that nature in any thing yealdeth, or Arte can compose./. This Stone excelleth in hardnes all Stones (*Diamond* excepted) and soe consequently in brightnes of watter as before argued, wch is proued when nature yealdeth him whitte, if he be well cutt he is matchable with any diamonds, especially of the greatter ones, for a great *diamond* is not so faire for his bignes commonly as a littel one, and a littel *Saphier* not so faire as a great one for his bignes / The reason is that the *Diamond* Cutter for sparing the Stone if it be great, will not cutt any away of his Circumference to giue his *diamond* full shape as he maye, and will doe a littel Stone, neither doeth nature giue to great ones (but rarely) anny such good proportion or thicknes to theire breadth, as haue the littel ones commonly, and this is generall both in Stone and pearle, the greater the worse proportioned, Therfore proportion giuen to a Stone by Arte, by the cuning Artificer helpeth nature, and addeth beautye as well as nature doeth, to the great commendations of that Misterye or Sience./. knowe this therfore that as the bade workman spoiles many a good Iuell both in cutting, pulishing, and also in the setting, Soe an excelent workman cann grace them aboue that wch nature giue them both in cutting, setting, and making them in valewe double of that they weare before, therfore he is better worthy of fowerfolde better payment then any other, though paraduenture (f.12*v*.) he doe it much soner, but commonly they are indeed longer about theire worke, wch maketh that they are poorer then the bunglers, ffor while the good workman taketh pleasure to shewe his art and Cuning aboue othe men in one peece (in what art soeuer) the botcher dispatches six or seauen, and giues it a good word or a boaste, keeping his promise within his time, wch greatly pleaseth most men, for indeed the tyme is all in most matters as sayet one, A thing well done out of due time is ill done, and soe hee getteth credit & custome wch keepeth thime, wherby he is able to set many other at work, wch though they be all bungler and Spoilers, yet please in respect of good cheapnes, and keeping of promise, and so growe rich./ the good Workman also wch crimson red, most like the kernels of very ripe pomegranate, which nature hath commended unto us in the ruby to be the principal red colour. Yet this little poor stone hath that special virtue to endure the fire, which none of the forenamed stones can do so well.

Sapphire blue

Now sapphire: whereof there be two kinds of colours white and blue, which blue is the most excellent perfect blue that nature in anything yieldeth, or art can compose. This stone excelleth in hardness all stones (diamond excepted), and so consequently in brightness of water, as before argued, which is proved when nature yieldeth him white. If he be well cut, he is matchable with any diamonds, especially of the greater ones, for a great diamond is not so fair for his bigness commonly as a little one, and a little sapphire not so fair as a great one for his bigness. The reason is that the diamond cutter, for sparing the stone, if it be great, will not cut away of his circumference to give his diamond full shape, as he may and will do a little stone. Neither doth nature give to great ones (but rarely) any such good proportion or thickness to their breadth as have the little ones commonly; and this is general both in stone and pearl, the greater the worse proportioned. Therefore proportion given to a stone by art, by the cunning artificer, helpeth nature and addeth beauty as well as nature doth, to the great commendation of that mystery or science.

Know this, therefore, that as the bad workman spoils many a good jewel, both in cutting, polishing, and also in the setting, so an excellent workman can grace them above that which nature gave them, both in cutting and setting, making them in value double of that they were before. Therefore he is better worthy of fourfold better payment than any other, though peradventure he do it much sooner. But commonly they are indeed longer about their work, which maketh that they are poorer than the bunglers: for while the good workman taketh pleasure to show his art and cunning above other men in one piece (in what art soever), the botcher dispatches six or seven, and gives it a good word or a boast, keeping his promise within his time, which greatly pleaseth most men, for indeed the time is all in most matters. As sayeth one: 'A thing well done out of due time is ill done;' and so he getteth credit and custom which keepeth time, whereby he is able to set many others at work, which, though they be all bunglers and spoilers, yet please in respect of good cheapness, and keeping of promise, and so grow rich. The good workman also which is so excellent is soe excelent, dependeth one his owne hand, and can hardly find any workmen to worke wth him, to heelpe him to keepe promise, and worke as well as himselfe, wch is a great mischeefe to him./. Neither is he alwayes in humore to imploye his spirits on some worke, but rather one some other, also such men are commonly noe Mysers, but liberall aboue theire littel degree, knowing howe bountifull god hath indued them wth skill aboue others, also they are much giuen to practises, to find out newe skills, and are euer trying conclusions, wch spendeth both theire time and mony, and oft times when they haue performed a rare pece of worke, (wch they indeede cannot afforde) they will giue it awaye to some worthy personage for very affecton, and to be spoken of, They are generally giuen to trauel, and to Confere with wise men, to fare meetly well, and to serue theire fantasies, hauing commonly many childeren if they be maryed./. A whch are causes of inpouerishment, if they be not stockt to receaue thereupon some profit by other trade, or that they be as in other countries by pencion or reward, of princes, otherwise vphelde and competently mayntayned, although they be neuer soe quicke nor soe cuninge in theire professions, depending but one theire owne hand helpe./. Thus much I thought neede to insert, in respect of the common opinion, or common slander (f.13*r.*) rather, wch is, that Cuning men are euer vnthrifts, and theerfor generally poore indede, when by the causes afore sayde they are fallen poore, they haue a more vnthrifty sheewe then others, for they will spend Still if they cann come buy it, soe that I thinke they haue the liberall Siences, and it is a vertue in them, and becometh them like men of vnderstanding./. If a man bring them a rare peece of worke, they will giue more for it, then most men of tenne times their abilitye, and in other countries they are Men of great wealth for the most parte./. Then yo to whome it apertaineth to knowe, may perceiue the reason in pte, why they are not so heere, the more is the pittye./.

Emerodde Well nowe for Greene, for certainly the *Emrod* is the most perfect greene on earth growing naturally, or that is in any thinge, or that is possible by Arte to make, (if it be an *Emerodd* of owld myne.) but rarely of the newe myne are they soe faire greene, for they are commonly paler as it weare mixed with seae greene, and *Eemerodd* of *Perooe* is of a thicke and troubled watter, there are in truth of theese three kinds of *Emrods*, of each kinde diuers cullors./. Noate also that of all the fiue precious Stones, there are some times white dependeth on his own hand, and can hardly find any workmen to work with him to help him to keep promise and work as well as himself, which is a great mischief to him. Neither is he always in humour to employ his spirits on some work, but rather on some other. Also, such men are commonly no misers, but liberal above their little degree, knowing how bountiful God hath endued them with skill above others; also, they are much given to practices to find out new skills, and are ever trying conclusions; which spendeth both their time and money. And oft-times, when they have performed a rare piece of work (which they indeed cannot afford) they will give it away to some worthy personage for very affection, and to be spoken of. They are generally given to travel, and to confer with wise men, to fare meetly well, and to serve their fancies, having commonly many children if they be married. All which are causes of impoverishment if they be not stocked to receive thereupon some profit by other trade, or that they be (as in other countries) by pension or reward of princes otherwise upheld and competently maintained, although they be never so quick nor so cunning in their professions, depending but on their own hands' help.

Thus much I thought need to insert in respect of the common opinion, or common slander rather, which is that cunning men are ever unthrifts, and therefore generally poor. Indeed, when by the causes aforesaid they are fallen poor, they have a more unthrifty show than others, for they will spend still if they can come by it; so that I think they love the liberal sciences, and it is a virtue in them, and becometh them like men of understanding. If a man bring them a rare piece of work they will give more for it than most men of ten times their ability. And in other countries they are men of great wealth for the most part. Then you to whom it appertaineth to know may perceive the reason in part why they are not so here, the more is the pity.

Emerald

Well now for green; for certainly the emerald is the most perfect green on earth growing naturally, or that is in anything, or that is possible by art to make, if it be an emerald of the old mine;[77] but rarely of the new mine are they so fair green, for they are commonly paler, as it were mixed with sea green; and emerald of Peru is of a thick and troubled water. There are in truth of these three kinds of emeralds, of each kind divers colours. Note also that of all the five precious stones there are sometimes ones, hauing no cullor at all, but Cleere as *Christall*, wch are better in regard of the rarety, then those wch haue cullor (except theire cullor be in perfection) and somtime there are found party cullored, as emrods the one halfe greene, and the other halfe pure cleare white, and soe likwise of all the otheres of the fyue Stones, such for the rarety are of the most price, and ought to be set soe, as one maye see the Stone one both Sides, to be the naturall Stone only, else it seemeth counterfeit by arte./. Ther are also sundry other greenish Stones, wch are no kind of emrods, nor soe good of vallue, namly *Griselite*, wch is popingey greene, *Egmeryne*, wch is a Sea greene, and *Burill*, wch is yet a more blweish greene, and are found very great, but if small, they be of small price or estimation./. I might well resemble these Stones vnto vs mankind, wherof Some be excelent and precious, and the common sort at first wiewe are like also vnto them, but if yo marke them weell, you (f.13*v*.) shall find them mixed cullors, dissembler softe Stones, not able to endure nor comprehend Scyence nor valorous deeds, and as a good Stone maye bee yll set, and ill vsed, soe that hee is Sould for naught: soe a good Seruant nor vsed in his kinde, falleth frome the Ignorant to a better master, and that as I said, If the base Stones be greeat, they are esteemed, whoe doubts of that, it is the like of me./.

Yeallowes Nowe of *Yeallowes*, the best is the *Topas orient*, or most perfect goold yeallowe, if this Stone want of his yeallownes, his vallue is the lesse (except hee be pure whit, and haue noe yellowe at all) for then resembleth he the *Diamond*, as dothe also the whit *Saphire*, wch is somwhat harder then the *Topas*, but very little./. *Topas* is better then white *Saphire* if it be naturaly whit, because it resembleth more the best watter of a *Diamond*, wch is to Incline a littell to yellowe, and will abyde to be sett and cutt on Tynne no the diamond myll, as the *Diamond* doth with diamond powder very well done./. And the yellow *Topas* which is but by Arte, as by fyer burnt white, will oftentimes returne to his perfect yellowe againe, a thinge admirable./. And a pale blewe *Saphire* wch hath a greenes in his blewe will neuer burne white, but rather recouer more blewnes, wch is greatly to be marueled att likwise, Thus haue I sufficiently proued the fyue principall cullors by the fyue precious Stones of most price (the *Diamond* excepted) wch properly is of no cullor, but a cleare watter cullor or Ayre cullor, so lucyde and bright, as hauing his due forme, his splendor or light is Somtimes called his fyer, and Somtimes his watter, by which his brightnes and his hardnes is knowne./. as for white ones, having no colour at all, but clear as crystal, which are better in regard of the rarity than those which have colour, except their colour be in perfection. And sometimes there are found parti-coloured, as emeralds the one half green and the other half pure clear white; and so likewise of all the others of the five stones. Such for the rarity are of the most price, and ought to be set so as one may see the stone on both sides to be the natural stone only, else it seemeth counterfeit by art. There are also sundry other greenish stones, which are no kind of emeralds, nor so good of value, namely chrysolite, which is popinjay green, aquamarine, which is a sea-green, and beryl, which is yet a more bluish green, and are found very great; but if small, they be of small price or estimation.

I might well resemble these stones unto us mankind, whereof some be excellent and precious, and the common sort at first view are like also unto them; but if you mark them well you shall find them mixed colours, dissembler soft stones, not able to endure nor comprehend science nor valorous deeds; and as a good stone may be ill set and ill used, so that he is sold for naught, so a good servant not used in his kind falleth from the ignorant to a better master. And that, as I said, if the base stones be great, they are esteemed, who doubts but that it is the like of men?[78]

Now of yellows: the best is the topaz orient, a most perfect gold yellow. *Yellows* If this stone want of his yellowness, his value is the less, except he be pure white, and have no yellow at all, for then resembleth he the diamond, as doth also the white sapphire, which is somewhat harder than the topaz, but very little. Topaz is better than white sapphire if it be naturally white, because it resembleth more the best water of a diamond, which is to incline a little to yellow; and will abide to be set and cut on tin on the diamond mill, as the diamond doth with diamond powder very well done. And the yellow topaz which is but by art (as by fire) burnt white will oftentimes return to his perfect yellow again, a thing admirable. And a pale blue sapphire which hath a greenness in his blue will never burn white, but rather recover more blueness, which is greatly to be marvelled at likewise.

Thus have I sufficiently proved the five principle colours by the five precious stones of most price, the diamond excepted, which properly is of no colour, but a clear water colour or air colour; so lucid and bright as, having his due form, his splendour or light is sometimes called his fire, and sometimes his water, by which his brightness and his hardness is excample, *Allome* or Sugar candy or gume are somewhat bright and hard, but not soe hard and bright as cristall / *Saphire* nothing so hard nor bright as *Diamond*, wch is indeede the brightest and therfore the hardest of all the precious Stones./ I haue discoursed at large, of all the perfect cullors wch are in the fyue Stones only, and aso of the other mixed cullors, wch are in all the other vnder Stones of softer and basser kinds, but now (as it weare in a *Ridle*) I demand what Stone is that wch hath (f.14*r*.) in it two distinct and perfect cullors very apparent, and hath in it noe cullor at all, yet if one looke longe into it, it hath many cullors radient and strange, but the *Diamond*./ And although white and blacke be both thicke cullors in painting, and not transparent, yet in the diamond they are cullors transparent and cleere, and wch may be counted amongst the transparent cullors both of whit and blacke, if whit and black weare counted cullors, as they are not./ wherfore I set them downe for no cullor, although indeede nothing hath his light more white, nor his shadowe more black, and being cleere, more cleerer then Ayre, yet being set on his black teyntor, or on any black pitch molten fast vnderneath vnto him, he changeth not his bright cleere whitnes, as any other Stone would doe, as *Topas*, *Saphiere*, *white Rubye*, or what soeuer, wch is a most admirable thinge to consider among the secretts in nature, and is the best waye to knowe a diamond frome an other Stone wthout hurting it./. This secret is not to be devulged, because stolne things are brought to sell, and therfore often times taken by his owne ignorantnes of the thinge hee offereth to sell, but the best hope is, they reade but fewe good bookes wch vse such facshions/..

Opall Now their is an other Stone wch hath all cullors in it selfe apparently, some blacke that are transparentt cullors namly the *Opall* wch in it hath a perfect fyer cullor, and all the cullors in the Raine bowe, though not placed in that order, but in a broken changable and retracted order, wch changeth his reflections wth euery turne through a sertaine cloudie cleere Milkeish whitnes lyke a   but the lesse it hath whitnes the better it is / This Stone is of a great value if he be great and fayre, and is equall for his bignes to anye Stone (*Diamond* and *Rubye* exceted) but is not much harder then pearle, and easely weareth rough / Ther is also another transparant Stone, which we call *Geratsolis* wch hath no cullors but a kynde of shyning, and if the Sune or sume bright daye light daye light weare vnder it or wthin it / *Turcas* wch is a thicke wached cullor, is also a good stone of price and estimation, and the Softest of thicke culored pecious known. As for example alum or sugar candy or gum are somewhat bright and hard, but not so hard and bright as crystal, so sapphire is nothing so hard and bright as diamond, which is indeed the brightest and therefore the hardest of all the precious stones.

I have discoursed at large of all the perfect colours which are in the five stones only, and also of the other mixed colours, which are in all the other under-stones of softer and baser kinds. But now (as it were in a riddle) I demand what stone is that which hath in it two distinct and perfect colours very apparent, and hath in it no colour at all, yet if one look into it it hath many colours radiant and strange, but the diamond? And although white and black be both thick colours in painting, and not transparent, yet in the diamond they are colours transparent and clear, and which may be counted amongst the transparent colours, both of white and black, if white and black were counted colours, as they are not. Wherefore I set them down for no colour, although indeed nothing hath his light more white nor his shadow more black; and being clear, more clearer than air, yet being set on his black tent,[79] or on any black pitch molten fast underneath unto him, he changeth not his bright clear whiteness, as any other stone would do – as topaz, sapphire, white ruby or whatsoever; which is a most admirable thing to consider among the secrets in nature, and is the best way to know a diamond from another stone without hurting it. This secret is not to be divulged, because stolen things are brought to sell, and therefore a thief is oftentimes taken by his own ignorance of the thing he offereth to sell; but the best hope is, they read but few good books, which use such fashions.

Now there is another stone which hath all colours in itself apparently, *Opal* including some blacks that are transparent colours; namely the opal, which in it hath a perfect fire colour, and all the colours in the rainbow, though not placed in that order, but in a broken, changeable and retracted order, which changeth his reflections with every turn through a certain cloudy-clear milkish whiteness, like a mist;[80] but the less it hath whiteness the better it is. This stone is of a great value if he be great and fair, and is equal for his bigness to any stone, diamond and ruby excepted; but is not much harder than pearl, and easily weareth rough. There is also another transparent stone, which we call girasol, which hath no colours, but a kind of shining; and if the sun or some bright daylight were under it or within it, is red. Turquoise, which is a thick watchet colour is also a good stone of price and estimation, and the softest of thick-coloured precious

Stones / The number wherof of Such Stones (f.14*v*.) are soe manye as weare longe to receite, wch I leaue therfore to speake of, as not soe needfull to the Treatise of perfect cullors, for they are all but mixed coullors./. wale/.

Howe to make the picture seeme to looke one in the face wch waie soe euer he goe or stand./.

Eauery man cannot possibly (though he haue the knowlege) doe euery worke he knowes, by reason of his naturall infermity of Complection, or humor, as for drawing vnder *Christall./*.

Mtr *Blanchgreene* for flowers of horne./.

Questions to be talked on./.

Wherof the Carnations are to be made, and howe the precious Stones and *Pearle* &c./.

In drawing after the life, site not nearer then too yards from the partye, and sit as euen of height as possible yo maye, but if hee be a very highe person, lett him sitte a littel aboue, because generally men be vnder him, and will soe Iuge of the picture, because they vnder wiewe him, if it be a very lowe person or childe vse the like discretion in placing him somewhat lower then yr selfe, If yo drawe frome head to foote, lett the party stand at least sixe yards frome yo, when yo take the discription of his whole stature, and so likwise for the stelling of yr picture / whate lenght soeuer, after yo haue proportioned the face, let the party arise, and stand, for in sitting, fewe cane sit very vpright as they stand, wherby the *Drawer* is greatly deceiued commonly, and the party drawne disgraced / tell not a body when yo drawe the hands, but when yo spie a good grace in theire hand take it quickly, or praye them to stand but still / for commonly when they are towld, they giue the hand the worse and more vnnaturall or affected grace, I would wish anybody to be well resolued wth themselues before hand, with what grace they would stand, and seeme, as though they neuer had resolued, nor weare to seeke, but take it without counsell./ –

the 18 of March 1624
Londres

stones. The number whereof of such stones are so many as were long to recite, which I leave therefore to speak of, as being not so needful to the treatise of perfect colours, for they are all but mixed colours.

Vale.

How to make the picture seem to look one in the face, which way soever he go or stand.

Every man cannot possibly (though he have the knowledge) do every work he knows, by reason of his natural infirmity of complexion or humour: as for example, drawing under crystal.[81]

Master Blanchgreene for flowers of horn.[82]

Questions to be talked on:

Whereof the carnations are to be made, and how the precious stones and pearls etc.

In drawing after the life, sit not nearer than two yards from the party, and sit as even of height as possibly you may; but if he be a very high person, let him sit a little above, because generally men be under him, and will so judge of the picture, because they under-view him. If it be a very low person or child, use the like discretion in placing him somewhat lower than yourself. If you draw from head to foot, let the party stand at least six yards from you when you take the description of his whole stature, and so likewise for the stelling[83] of your picture, what length soever. After you have proportioned the face, let the party arise and stand, for in sitting few can sit very upright as they stand, whereby the drawer is greatly deceived, and commonly the party drawn disgraced. Tell not a body when you draw the hands, but when you spy a good grace in their hand take it quickly, or pray them to stand but still; for commonly when they are told, they give the hand the worse and more unnatural or affected grace. I would wish anybody to be well resolved with themselves beforehand with what grace they would stand, and seem as though they never had resolved, nor were to seek, but take it without counsel.

The 18th of March, 1624
Londres.

(f.15*r*.) A more Compendious discourse concerning ye art of Liming the natture and properties of the Coullers,

Whits

To proceed & begine wth ye Coullers, Whitt ffor it's Virgin puritie is the most Exellent, viz:t Ceruse & whitt Lead, both subiect to Inconueniencies and are thus preuented The Cerusse (affter you haue wrought itt,) will tarnish, and many tims looke of a Redish or yeallowish Couller, The whitt-lead, iff to much ground will glister or shine & iff you grind itt to Course will bee vnfitt to worke & so vnseruicable,/ Ther is but on way to remidy itt, wch is to Lay them in ye sunn to or three days before you grind yem w:ch will Exhalle and draw away those sallt and gressie mixtures, ytt starue and poyson the Coull:s besids you must scrape Away the superfices of the whitt Lead and only vuse the purest of itt put to this as to all yor Coull:s a Littell gume Arabeck of the best and whittest w:ch you must haue by you in a littell box, made into very fine powder or elce disolued into watter, as you please, and with a few drops of fair runing watter temper itt with yor finger till the gume be Incorporated or disolued The gume must bee vs'd att discretion, yor owne practice will Informe you ye best, for no Generall rulle can be giuen, only leaue not your Coullers to moist & reliqued but some whatt thike & Clamy & then Couer itt Cleane frome the dust till itt bee dry in the shell, and then if itt bee not to much, nor, to littell, bound, you will find itt, iff to much itt will glissen, iff to Littell, drawing yor finger ouer itt some of the Couller will come off / India Lake to be ground w:th Gume watter, and spread thine About the shell, Vmber and some other Coullers much subject to crakle & fall frome the shell in pieces, when you find itt so take allittell whitt sugar Candy reduced in to fine powder and with a few drops of fair watter, you must temper the Couller Againe as itt is in the shell till both the Coullers & the suggar Candy be throughly disollued, w:ch being once dry will lye fast in the shell English Oker will lye fast in the shell, & workes well iff well ground, Pink is allso A very good Couller and workes sharpe and neatt, and must be ground as ye Rest; Vmber being A fowle and gressie Couller, iff when you haue bought itt you burne itt in A Crusible or Goldsmiths pott, itt is Clensed & being ground as the Rest, workes well, Tera de Collana is easie to worke when itt is new

The grinding of yor Coullers

A More Compendious Discourse Concerning the Art of Limning, the Nature and Properties of the Colours

To proceed and begin with the colours: white for its virgin purity is the most excellent, viz. ceruse and white lead; both are subject to inconveniences, and are thus prevented: the ceruse, after you have wrought it, will tarnish, and many times look of a reddish or yellowish colour; the white lead, if too much ground, will glister or shine, and if you grind it too coarse will be unfit to work, and so unserviceable. There is but one way to remedy it, which is to lay them in the sun two or three days before you grind them, which will exhale and draw away those salt and greasy mixtures that starve and poison the colours. Besides, you must scrape away the superficies of the white lead, and only use the purest of it. Put to this, as to all your colours, a little gum arabic of the best and whitest, which you must have by you in a little box, made into very fine powder or else dissolved into water, as you please; and with a few drops of fair running water temper it with your finger till the gum be incorporated or dissolved. The gum must be used at discretion; your own practice will inform you the best, for no general rule can be given. Only leave not your colour too moist and too liquid,[84] but somewhat thick and clammy, and then cover it clean from the dust till it be dry in the shell, and not too much nor too little bound; you will find that if too much it will glisten; if too little, drawing your finger over it some of the colour will come off.

Whites

India lake to be ground with gum water and spread thin about the shell; umber and some other colours are much subject to crackle and fall from the shell in pieces. When you find it so, take a little white sugar candy reduced into fine powder, and with a few drops of fair water you must temper the colour again as it is in the shell, till both the colour and the sugar candy be thoroughly dissolved; which, being once dry, will lie fast in the shell. English ochre will lie fast in the shell, and works well if well ground. Pink is also a very good colour, and works sharp and neat, and must be ground as the rest. Umber, being a foul and greasy colour, if when you have bought it you burn it in a crucible or goldsmith's pot, it is cleansed, and being ground as the rest works well. Terra de Collana is easy to work when it is new ground, and is very good to close up the

The grinding of your colours

grownd and is very good to Close vp the Last & deepest touches in the shadowed places of picturs, by ye Liffe. Cheristone and Iuory ard both to bee burned & so ground, the first is a very good blak especially for drapperies and blake Aparell, but if you mak sattin itt must be tempered with A Littell India Lake & Indico but only to make itt apeere w:th A more beautifull Glose, w:ch Heightned w:th a Littell lighter mixtur of more whittish in strong touches & Hard reflections, and deep'ned w:th Iuory will shew maruellous well, Iuory blake must be well tempered w:th suggar Candy To preuent Craking,/ But befor I begine I will shew you the reson why thes Coullers must be washed, w:ch is because thay are of A sandy Loose & & grauely quallitie & so heauy & ponderous & sollide bodies ytt thay will hardly be Reduced to that finenesse, requierable in this art, for iff you thinke to make them fine by grinding thay will Instantly Loose ther beawtie, To Refine yem therfore by washing, you are to take of Red Lead w:ch is the first in number About an ounce or tow iff you please and puting itt in a littell basson or such Like of Clear watter, stire itt for a whille to Geather either wth yor hand or some spoone, till you see the watter all Coullered & stained w:th the Couller, then Lett itt stand a whille, and you will perceaue on the vper face of ye watter A Gressy skome Arise, w:ch togather w:th all the watter powr out and cast away, then fill you basson with fresh watter and stirr itt as before w:ch done before the watter be halfe settled powre itt into an other clean porrenger or such Lik, reseruing behind in the first bason the dreggs & settling of the Coullers, w:ch may be the greattest p.te (f.15*v.*) yet Itt is to be cast away for much is not that you are to seeke but good for a Littell in any Couller goes far in Limning, And if a Handfull of Red Lead yeeald a shell or tow of good Coull:r itt is Enough so itt be fine, The coull:d & trubled watter as I sayed before, being in a second dish, Ade more watter ther to, and wash them well to geather as before, w:ch done Lett itt settle till the watter be Allmost cleare, iff you perceaue the skume arise still vpon the watter, powre itt of still, till the watter be cleare, for ye skume is chalke or other filth in the Coull:r w:ch you are to cast of by stirring itt, (I mean) all the Coul:r to geather then sufering itt to settle, and as Longe as the skume ariseth still powr itt A way, Itt will not be a misse iff when you haue wast yor Coull:r a whille & stirring the watter till a gaine itt become thike, you powre out halfe of that thickned watter into A third dish, and washin both ye second & the third you will find you

To make Sattin

to wash Coullers

How to wash Coullers

last and deepest touches in the shadowed places of pictures by the life. Cherry stone and ivory are both to be burned and so ground; the first is a very good black, especially for draperies and black apparel, but if you make satin it must be tempered with a little India lake or indigo, but only to make it appear with a more beautiful gloss, which heightened with a little lighter mixture of more whiteish in strong touches and hard reflections, and deepened with ivory will show marvellous well. Ivory black must be well tempered with sugar candy to prevent cracking. *To make satin*

But before I begin, I will show you the reason why these colours must be washed, which is because they are of a sandy, loose and gravelly quality, and so heavy and ponderous and solid bodies that they will hardly be reduced to that fineness requirable in this art; for if you think to make them fine by grinding, they will instantly lose their beauty. To refine them therefore by washing, you are to take of red lead, which is the first in number, about an ounce, or two if you please, and putting it in a little basin or such like of clear water, stir it for a while together, either with your hand or some spoon, till you see the water all coloured and stained with the colour. Then let it stand a while, and you will perceive on the upper face of the water a greasy scum arise, which, together with all the water, pour out and cast away. Then fill your basin with fresh water, and stir it as before; which done, before the water be half settled, pour it into another clean porringer or such like, reserving behind in the first basin the dregs and settling of the colours, which may be the greatest part. Yet it is to be cast away, for much is not that you are to seek, but good; for a little in any colour goes far in limning, and if a handful of red lead yield a shell or two of good colour it is enough, so it be fine. The coloured and troubled water, as I said before being in a second dish, add more water thereto, and wash them well together as before; which done let it settle till the water be almost clear. If you perceive the scum arise still upon the water, pour it off still, till the water be clear, for the scum is chalk or other filth in the colour, which you are to cast off by stirring it (I mean all the colour together), then suffering it to settle, and as long as the scum ariseth, still pour it away. It will not be amiss if, when you have washed your colour a while, and stirring the water till again it became thick, you pour out half of that thickened water into a third dish, and washing both the second and the third, you will *To wash colours* *How to wash colours* couler of a courser and finer quallitie, Insomuch as the third & iff you please ye 4:th and 5:th sort will be very fine, and faire, when you haue well washed Them often & by Continuall Changing and shifting the watters & Coull:rs You find itt perfectly Clensed, you must by littell and littell Gently draw away ye Remaine of ye watter, not sufering any or aery littell of the Coull:r to goe away with itt, so that setting yor dishes in the sunn & sheluing them one the one side, you will find yor Coull:r dryed and Lying A bout the sids of the dishes, like drifts of sand, in some places you will find itt faire & cleare and fine, and in other more course and fowle, when itt is all through dryed take away with yor finger or feather the finest p:te of the Couller, wch will Like fine flower fall away wth the Least touch, Reserue itt for yor vse ye Courser sort you may keepe for ordinary worke, But when you vse this Couller you must take as much as will lye in ashell I meane only to spread About the side of ashell somwhatt thinne, that you may Handsomly take itt of with your pencill, w:ch you can not conueniently doe if you fill your shell full, or lett itt lie thike or on Heaps, and wth Gume watter or gume in Powlder (as I sayed before,) w:th a few drops of watter, tempr itt finely w:th yr finger and Lett itt spread a bout the sids of ye shells, as you did in yor other Ground Coll:rs for yor Pencills, must be well chosen cleane and sharpe, pointed not deuiding in to p:ts full & thike towards the quill, & so decending to A Round and sharp point I preferre thesse before yem that are Longe & slender as Retaining the Couller Longer & deliuering Itt out more free and flowing then the other, iff any haire is Longer then the Rest take itt off w:th asharp pen-kniff, or passe itt through the fflame of a Candle, the Pencills you vse in Gold or silluer you are to Reserue for thatt purpose and not to mix or temper with other Coullers.

For Yo:r Pencills

Itt may be ouall, or square, as you will, or the partie drawne desirs itt Take an ordinary playing Card, pollish itt and make itt so smoth as possible you can, ye whitt side of itt, make itt eury wheare euen, and clean frome spots, then chuse the best abortiue Parchment & Cutting out A peece Equall to yor Card, w:th fine and Cleane starch past itt on the Card wch done Lett itt dry then making yor Grind stone as Cleane as may bee, lay the Card on the stone, the parchment sid downeward, and then Pollish itt well on the backe sid Itt will make much the smother, you must past yor pchment so that the out side of the skinn may be outward Itt being the smothest and best side to worke on, (f.16*r*.)

for yor Table or Carde,

find your colour of a coarser and finer quality, insomuch as the third (and, if you please, the fourth and fifth) sort will be very fine and fair. When you have well washed them often, and by continual changing and shifting the waters and colours you find it perfectly cleansed, you must by little and little gently draw away the remains of the water, not suffering any, or very little, of the colour to go away with it. So that setting your dishes in the sun and shelving them on the one side, you will find your colour dried, and lying about the sides of the dishes like drifts of sand. In some places you will find it fair and clear and fine, and in others more coarse and foul. When it is all through dried, take away with your finger or a feather the finest part of the colour, which will, like fine flour, fall away with the least touch; reserve it for your use. The coarser sort you may keep for ordinary work. But when you use this colour, you must take as much as will lie in a shell; I mean only to spread about the side of a shell somewhat thin, that you may handsomely take it off with your pencil, which you cannot conveniently do if you fill your shell full, or let it lie thick or in heaps. And with gum water or gum in powder (as I said before) with a few drops of water temper it finely with your finger and let it spread about the sides of the shells as you did in your other ground colours.

For your pencils

For your pencils, they must be well chosen, clean and sharp pointed, not dividing in two parts, full and thick towards the quill, and so descending to a round and sharp point. I prefer these before them that are long and slender, as retaining the colour longer and delivering it out more free and flowing than the other. If any hair is longer than the rest take it off with a sharp pen knife, or pass it through the flame of a candle. The pencils you use in gold or silver you are to reserve for that purpose, and not to mix or temper with other colours.

For your table or card

It may be oval or square as you will, or as the party drawn desires it. Take an ordinary playing card, polish it, and make it so smooth as possibly you can (the white side of it); make it everywhere even and clean from spots, then choose the best abortive parchment, and cutting out a piece equal to your card, with fine and clean starch paste it on the card. Which done, let it dry; then making your grindstone as clean as may be, lay the card on the stone, the parchment side downward, and then polish it well on the back side; it will make it much the smoother. You must paste your parchment so that the outside of the skin may be outward, it being the smoothest and best side to work on.

To lay yor ground You are to lay yor ground, or Primer, of a flesh Coll:r so neer as you can, of the same Complexion the p:tie is, rather somwhatt fairer, for by shadowing you can make itt browner att pleasure, for in Limning you must neuer heighten but worke itt downe to ye Iust Coll:r hauing ppared yor Coll:r you Remenbr to fill yor Pencill full of Coll:r rather thinn & watterish then thicke & grose, and w:th to or three sweeps or dashes w:th a bigger then ordinarie Pencill: lay itt on in an Instant for the sooner you doe itt, the better and euener will yor Collr Lye and forgett not to Couer so much or more of yor Card then you meane to make the face because that if you should happen to Lay the ground to Littell you will very hardly add any more onto itt, but very vneuen And not suttable to the rest, Therfore all must be done att once and speedily for iff you be Longe in Laying this Complexion the Card or rather pchment will roughell or risse and Come frome the Card.

To tempr yor Collrs This done you are to take a pretty large shell off Mother of Pearlle or such like and before you begin to worke you must temper certaine littlle heaps of seuerall shadows for the face w:ch as the oyle Painters lay on ther woden Pallats in like maner you must Lay them ready ppared in order by themselues about The border or Circomferance of the shells/.

How to work yor first Coll: The first Coullers you are to begine the face w:th are Red, that is to say of the Cheeks and lipps somwhat strongly in the bottome of the Chinne if the p:tie be beardlesse as allso ouer, vnder and about the eyes you will pceaue a dellicate and faint rednes About the eies somwhat Inclining to A purple, w:ch in faire and beawtifull faces is ordinary and must be obserued dilligently, all this you must worke affter the maner of washing or hatching, drawing yor Pencill along and with faint & Gentle stroaks or rather washing or wipping then with pricks to Prick and Punch itt as some doe affech, In yor dead Coulloring you need not be exactt and curious but rather bold and Iuditious, for though yor worke Appeers rough att first yett in the finishing yor worke will be in yor owne Power and Pleasure to sweeten & Close itt as neat & Curiously as you will: Yor next worke is the faint & blew shadows About The eys the Corners and balls of them, and Grayish & blewish shadows About ye temples w:ch you are to worke frome the vper parte of the face, exceeding sweett & faint by degrees, The fainter and lighter shadows being done & some whatt smothed and wrought into the red, you may goe ouer *for yor haire,* yor Haire, you must first draw them with Collo:r as neere as you

You are to lay your ground or primer of a flesh colour so near as you can of the same complexion the party is, rather somewhat fairer; for by shadowing you can make it browner at pleasure, for in limning you must never heighten, but work it down to the just colour. Having prepared your colour, you remember to fill your pencil full of colour, rather thin and waterish than thick and gross; and with two or three sweeps or dashes, with a bigger than ordinary pencil, lay it on in an instant, for the sooner you do it, the better and evener will your colour lie. And forget not to cover so much or more of your card than you mean to make the face, because that if you should happen to lay the ground too little, you will very hardly add any more on to it, but very uneven, and not suitable to the rest. Therefore all must be done at once and speedily, for if you be long in laying this complexion, the card, or rather parchment, will ruffle or rise, and come from the card. *To lay your ground*

This done, you are to take a pretty large shell of mother of pearl or such like, and before you begin to work you must temper certain little heaps of several shadows for the face, which, as the oil painters lay on their wooden palettes, in like manner you must lay them ready prepared in order by themselves about the border or circumference of the shells. *To temper your colours*

The first colours you are to begin the face with are red; that is to say, of the cheeks and lips somewhat strongly, in the bottom of the chin if the party be beardless, as also over, under, and about the eyes. You will perceive a delicate and faint redness about the eyes, somewhat inclining to a purple, which in fair and beautiful faces is ordinary, and must be observed diligently. All this you must work after the manner of washing or hatching, drawing your pencil along and with faint and gentle strokes, or rather washing or wiping rather than with pricks to prick and punch it, as some do affect.[85] In your dead colouring you need not be exact and curious, but rather bold and judicious; for though your work appears rough at first, yet in the finishing your work will be in your own power and pleasure to sweeten and close it as neat and curious as you will. Your next work is the faint and blue shadows about the eyes, the corners and balls of them, and greyish and blueish shadows about the temples, which you are to work from the upper part of the face, exceeding sweet and faint by degrees. The fainter and lighter shadows being done, and somewhat smoothed and wrought into the red, you may go over your hair; *How to work your first colours* *For your hair* can suttable to the Life, and afterward wash then roughly as the rest/

To make Armor, Yor Armour Layd Liquid silluer flatt & euen w:ch dryed and burnished w:th a small Wessells tooth handsomly ffitted into a pensill stick then temp:r the shadow for yor Armour w:th silluer Littmus and A littell vmber, and worke yor shadows vpon & ouer the silluer acording to the obserutions in the Liffe the burnisht siluer to be Left for the heightnings, the deepnings, must be ye deepest of yor shadows, the thinner p:te whearof wth sume store of silluer, must bee sweetly & neatly wrought into ye silluer layd all *for Gold* flatt before, As for Gold you may Lay your ground flatt with English *oaker* tempered with Liqued gold yett there is, a stone growing in the oxes gall w:ch thay call a *gall-stone* w:ch is Ground & tempered w:th gold is of exelent Luster, & beawtie, in the shadowing of which, in the deeppest & darkest places, must be mixed A littell Blake, the hightning must be the finest and purest gold (I meane Liqued,) Iff in yor gold worke ther be any Caruing or Imbosiing and that in ye Lighter p:ts itt must be sparkling & pleasant:

you must first draw them with colour as near as you can suitable to the life, and afterward wash them roughly as the rest.

To make armour

Your armour laid liquid silver, flat and even, which, dried and burnished with a small weasel's tooth handsomely fitted into a pencil stick; then temper the shadow for your armour with silver, litmus, and a little umber, and work your shadows upon and over the silver according to the observations in the life. The burnished silver to be left for the heightenings; the deepenings must be the deepest of your shadows, the thinner part whereof with some store of silver must be sweetly and neatly wrought into the silver laid all flat as before.

For gold

As for gold, you may lay your ground flat with English ochre tempered with liquid gold; yet there is a stone growing in the ox's gall which they call a gall-stone, which if ground and tempered with gold is of excellent lustre and beauty; in the shadowing of which in the deepest and darkest places must be mixed a little black. The heightening must be the finest and purest gold (I mean liquid). If in your gold work there be any carving or embossing, and that in the lighter parts, it must be sparkling and pleasant.

NOTES

1. For a discussion of Haydocke, see Karl J. Höltgen, 'Richard Haydocke: Translator, Engraver, Physician', *The Library*, XXXIII (1978), 15–32.

2. Quoted by F. B. Troup, 'Biography of John Bodley, Father of Sir Thomas Bodley', *Transactions of the Devonshire Association*, XXXV (1903), 167–197 (p.179).

3. Ibid, p.187.

4. Later in Hilliard's career, connections with Thomas Bodley, his near contemporary in the Bodley household, occur in a way that may be more than coincidental: both men travelled to France in the same year, 1576, while in 1598, when Bodley was most actively engaged in the foundation of the great library, Hilliard painted his portrait. In the same year Haydocke dedicated his translation of Lomazzo to Bodley; it is quite conceivable that Bodley was a link between the Oxford physician and virtuoso and the London miniaturist, and had some hand in the genesis of the *Treatise*.

5. See also Pope-Hennessy, p.99: 'there is little doubt that the Elizabethan would have regarded both portrait and frame as a single unit, an enamelled jewel containing a limned likeness'.

6. Hilliard may be thinking of *verre eglomisé* when he refers in a note at the end of the *Treatise* to 'drawing under crystal'. See p.95.

7. See, for example, Graham Reynolds's review of Colding, *Burlington Magazine*, XCVII (1955), p.58.

8. For a detailed account of the work carried out by the Serjeant Painters, see Erna Auerbach, *Tudor Artists* (1954), pp.107–119.

9. The reader may wish to be reminded of the dates of Hans Holbein the Younger (1497/8–1543), of the dates of his visit to England in 1526, of his return to Switzerland in 1528 and his return to England in 1532. He is said to have learnt the art of limning during the 1530s from another foreign artist resident in London, Lucas Horenboult.

10. 'New Light on Jacobean Painters', *Burlington Magazine*, CXVIII (1976), 74–83.

11. It may be more than a coincidence that the other blocks cut by 'C.T.' are based on a design by someone with Robert Brandon's initials: see McKerrow and Ferguson, facs. 143, 144 and 152.

12. *Arte de la pintura*, 1638, ed. F. J. Sanchez Canton (Madrid, 1956), II, p.36.

13. See Roy Strong, *The Cult of Elizabeth* (1977), pp.57–60. Strong also suggests that Hilliard was influenced by other artists of the Valois court, particularly the anonymous Maître de Flore.

14. Letter to John Ray, 22 Oct. 1691. Ray's reply praises Samuel Cooper: 'for that kind of painting he was esteemed the best artist in Europe'. Quoted by Anthony Powell, *John Aubrey and His Friends* (1948), pp.217–8. The miniature was stolen from the Ashmolean in 1691.

15. Another Nicholas Hilliard, with a wife and two children, is mentioned in the will, now lost, made in 1631 by Hilliard's brother, Jeremy, a goldsmith in Exeter. The relationship of this Nicholas to Jeremy is not made clear in the abstract of the will in the West Country Studies Library (O. Murray collection, 8.37), but he does not seem to have been a London goldsmith, and is therefore less likely than the elder Nicholas Hilliard to have married the daughter or widow of another London goldsmith.

16. Bate adds some material to the drawing of the face (see p.61): 'First draw the stroake for the fore head, which must be done most exactly, because that according unto that scantling and proportion, must all the rest be drawne; as if the fore-head be so long, then from the forehead to the chin, must be twice so long; next draw the farthest eye; thirdly draw the nose, fourthly draw the nearest eye, leaving the just length of an eye between it and the other; having continuall regard that the parties farthest eye, seen to your appearing to bee just so much distant from the forehead stroake, as it was when you first began; if it be not, proceed no farther until you have recovered, or recalled him to his former place, then draw the mouth, next the chin, then finish the out line of the face; and lastly the haire: having finished the head, draw the whole bodie proportionable thereunto' (*The Mysteries of Nature and Art*, 2nd edition, 1635, pp.149–50). He also adds material to the passage which proceeds from the laying of carnations: 'To draw the trace after the carnation is layd, and to give the red to the cheeks, take lake and vermilion, and for to give the light, take *Venice* ceruse only, for an old man adde a little oker unto it, for the shadowes take a little black and lake, but for a woman make it very white, for an old man take the other shadowes and a little soot, for the last shadow for the compassing of the face, take lake a little black, with some russet oker, and soot; as for the hayre, it must be shadowed according unto the colour thereof' (Ibid, p.203).

17. Passages in square brackets in the transcript are Vertue's additions; we have retained them here because it is quite possible that he had some

knowledge of the missing passages. His marginalia, distinguished from the original marginalia which are in italics, are retained in the transcript, but omitted in the modernised text.

18. Paolo Lomazzo (1538–1600), Milanese art theorist and painter. Becoming blind at 33 he turned from painting to writing, publishing his *Trattato dell'arte della pittura, scoltura ed architettura*, the so-called 'bible of mannerism', in 1584. Haydocke translated the first five books into English, and Hilliard shows his familiarity with Haydocke's translation rather than the Italian original.

19. i.e. which the surface involved can bear, or is adapted to receive (see *OED* under 'charge', v.4).

20. The reference to Ecclesiasticus is a little misleading; the texts which are most directly referred to in this passage are Exodus 31.1–6 and Exodus 35.30–35, from which the conjectural additions to the modernised text are partly drawn. The passages are commonly cited in contemporary defences of art, as in Henry Peacham, *The Gentlemans Exercise* (1612), p.1, and in John Case's introductory epistle 'To his Friende *R.H.* of New Colledge' in Haydocke. Ecclesiasticus does however contain related matter, to which Hilliard may be alluding. Ecclesiasticus 38.24, for example, says that 'The wisdom of a learned man cometh by opportunity of leisure', while 39.4 says that the wise man will 'appear before princes'; but the whole context is rich in relevant material. Hilliard is not quoting directly from any of the several English translations available to him.

21. 'Recognition sustains the arts'. Cicero, *Tusculan Disputations*, I.ii.4.

22. See Haydocke, *The First Booke: of Proportion*, pp.8 and 14.

23. Roman painter of *c.*300 B.C., described by Cicero as 'of noble family' (*Tusculan Disputations*, I.ii.4); cf. Peacham, *The Gentlemans Exercise*, p.3 and Baldassare Castiglione, *The Book of the Courtier*, translated T. Hoby (Everyman's Library, 1928), p.77.

24. *Pamitius* is almost certainly a copyist's error. Hilliard probably wrote 'Patricius', referring to Francesco Patrizi, Bishop of Gaeta (1413–1494), whose widely known *De institutione reipublicae* (Paris, 1518) discusses the place of painting and sculpture in the commonwealth (I.x); Patrizi refers just as Hilliard does, first to Quintus Fabius and then to Marcus Aurelius and his painter, although he cannot be said to be 'reckoning up' Marcus's attendants, other than his teachers:

'Non puduit Fabium Patricium illum Romanum optimo genere oriundum, qui maiorum suorum nobilitatem ab Hercule vsque recensebat, pictura exerceri, & ab ea cognomentum accipere. Nec diu post pœnituit Marcum Antoninum doctissimum ac sanctissimum

Imperatorem operam picturæ dare sub Diogene praeceptore, quamquam illustrioribus disciplinis indulgebat, & magistris quibusque eruditissimis vtebatur' (Argentinae, 1594 edition, p.54).

Another possible candidate for 'Pamitius' is the Veronese antiquarian Onofrio Panvinio (1529–1568), whose many works contain lists of those 'attendant upon' Emperors, though we have found none to fit this particular context. The painting master Diognetus is first mentioned briefly by 'Julius Capitolinus' in the life of Marcus Aurelius in the *Historia Augusta* (IV.9), while a Diognetus is mentioned by Marcus himself as one of his principal mentors in the *Meditations* (I.iii).

25. Strictly, paintings of historical subjects, but by Hilliard's time the term covered any painting containing figures.

26. This is by far the fullest account we have of Bossam, none of whose work is known to survive. A reading minister was one who merely read the lessons or service, without preaching.

27. Albrecht Dürer (1471–1528), like Hilliard the son of a master goldsmith, spent the last three years of his life working on his theoretical writings: the *Treatise of Measurement* (1525), the *Introduction on Fortification* (1527) and the *Four Books on Human Proportion* (1528). Like most of the artists in the *Treatise*, he would have been best known to Hilliard as an engraver, but his writings were available in Latin and, by 1557, the *Four Books on Human Proportion*, with which Hilliard seems most familiar, were translated into French.

28. Hendrick Goltzius (1558–1616), the greatest line engraver of his generation. He worked in Haarlem from 1576, and visited Germany and Italy in 1590–91. In 1586 he engraved a fine medal of the Earl of Leicester, then in the Netherlands.

29. Lucas van Leyden (1494–1533), precocious painter and engraver. He was much influenced by Dürer whom he met in 1521, and was one of the major graphic artists of his period. He was said to have a predilection for yellow silk clothes, and to have done much of his work in bed.

30. Engraving tool.

31. Haydocke, *The Fifthe Booke: of Perspective*, p.205 (a direct quotation). See also ibid., p.181.

32. 'Quam multa vident pictores in umbris et in eminentia, quae nos non videmus!' Cicero, *Academica Priora*, II, 20.

33. He never does develop this argument, for which see Haydocke, *The First Booke: of Proportion*, pp.4–6 and 18–19, Castiglione, pp.78–81, and Pope-Hennessy, p.92.

34. Hilliard was wrong in thinking that Dürer had not been to Italy.

35. *Rosso:* probably Giambattista Rossi (1494–1541), Florentine painter, designer and engraver. As well as his engravings, Hilliard may have seen his major work as a painter in the Palace of Fontainebleau.

36. *Lambertus Suavius:* Lambert Zutman (1510?–1575?) Flemish engraver, painter, printer, poet and architect. He had a workshop at Antwerp in the 1550s. Hilliard may have come across him during his early travels with Bodley. He was the son of the goldsmith Henri Zutman.

37. Possibly meaning 'loose-fitting'; although *OED* does not record this usage until 1893 (under 'straight', A adj. 2j), the fact that it appears then as a professional term used by tailors suggests that it may well have survived unrecorded over several centuries. It makes more obvious sense here than 'strait' meaning 'tight-fitting', the normal meaning in Elizabethan times.

38. Not the modern lead pencil, but a paint brush. See the introductory section on 'The Technique of Miniature Painting'.

39. The naked skin.

40. William Camden's account in his *Remains Concerning Britain* provides the most succinct and authoritative distinction. Under 'Impresses' he writes: 'An Impress (as the Italians call it) is a device in Picture with his Motto, or Word, born by Noble and Learned Parsonages, to notifie some particular conceit of their own, as Emblems (that we may omit other differences) do propound some general instruction to all . . . There is required in an Impress . . . a correspondency of the picture which is as the body; and the Motto, which as the soul giveth it life.'

41. Pope-Hennessy rightly calls attention to the similarity of Bacon's treatment of *favour* in the essay on Beauty, which has the same triple hierarchy: 'In beauty, that of favour is more than that of colour, and that of decent and gracious motion more than that of favour.'

42. This rather rhetorical and somewhat detached passage is not a direct quotation from the Bible, but does have much in common with the Wisdom of Solomon, especially 7.24, which in the Douay version reads: 'For wisdom, is more active than all active things; and reacheth every where by reason of her purity.'

43. A standard of measurement or estimation (see also note 16).

44. The addition of *not* is supported by the version of this passage in *A Drawing Book*.

45. Sir Christopher Hatton (1540–1591), first attracted Elizabeth's attention at a court masque and 'danced into her favour', becoming a gentleman pensioner and, in 1572, captain of her bodyguard. He was perhaps closer to Elizabeth than anyone except Leicester, and became

her Lord Chancellor in 1587.

46. William Hogarth's drawing of Quin and Garrick deals with a related problem in 1746: 'If the exact Figure of Mr Quin, were to be reduc'd to the size of the print of Mr Garrick it would seem to be the shortest man of the two, because Mr Garrick is of a taller proportion.' See plate 61 of *English Drawings. Stuart and Georgian Periods. In the Collection of His Majesty the King at Windsor Castle* by A. P. Oppé (1950).

47. The author in question is Sir John Harington in *Ariosto's Orlando Furioso in English Heroical Verse* (1591): 'we have with us at this day, one that for limning (which I take to be the verie perfection of that art) is comparable with any of any other country . . . I thinke our countryman (I meane Mr. Hilliard) is inferior to none that lives at this day: as among other things of his doing, myselfe have seen him, in white and blacke in four lynes only, set downe the feature of the Queenes Majesties countenance: that it was ever hereby to be knowne; and he is so perfect therein (as I have heard others tell) that he can set it down by the Idea he hath, without any patterne.' (pp.277–8).

48. For the probable origins of this notion in an incident related by Pliny, via the mannerist theorist Armenini's *De' veri precetti della pittura* (Ravenna, 1587), see Pope-Hennessy, p.96.

49. Compare Haydocke, *The Fourth Booke: of Light:* 'having lights well disposed, it doth not only adde perfection to the draught, but so *sets it off from the flat*, that it seemes to be imbossed.' (p.135; Haydocke's italics).

50. i.e. the wish to assume some particular symbolic pose. For a carefully-researched but unconvincingly argued discussion of a Hilliard miniature based on a 'special device or affection of the stander', see Leslie Hotson, *Shakespeare by Hilliard: a Portrait Deciphered* (1977).

51. See Haydocke, *The Fourth Booke: of Light*, p.138: 'for the shaddowes doe necessarily follow the lights, being caused by the decay of the light,' and p.176: 'shaddowes are as it were the tayle of Light.'

52. For details of the colour names and the nature of the pigments see the 'Note on Colours' in the Introduction. Although Hilliard's preliminary dismissal of certain colours does not completely accord with his later inclusion of some of them, it was the usual practice to begin with a catalogue of colours and a list of those unsuitable for limning. Norgate in *Miniatura* (p.7) writes that 'In this Catalogue of Colours I doe purposely omit Brazill, Verdigreece, Orpiment, Rosett, Turnsole, Litmus, Logwood, and others, as not worthy the naming, nor by reason of their course and grosse Body, their dangerous qualitie, some beinge mineralls, nor their Cheapnes and Comunity, to be used at all in this cleanly neat, and exquesite Art, being indeed fitter for those that wash prints or coulour Mapps then to be admitted into our Company'. And

Alexander Browne has a similar list and dismissal in *The Whole Art of Drawing* (1660), p.8.

53. For a similar list of basic colours, see Peacham, *The Compleat Gentleman*, pp.154–9, and Haydocke, *The Third Booke: of Colours*, p.98: 'Now there be 7 sortes of simple colours, from which all the rest arise. Of these two are extreames, as *white & Blacke*; and 5 middle, as *light yeallow, redde, purple, Blewe* and *Greene.*' Pope-Hennessy notes the similarity of this list to those of other mannerist theorists (p.97). Hilliard is distinct from both Peacham and Norgate in that he goes out of his way to emphasise that purple is 'not a proper colour' (see p.83) and, indeed, Thompson asserts that 'Colours which we should ordinarily call purple now are not very common in medieval painting' (p.159).

54. The reading *Item* is from *A Drawing Book*, though both *iter* and *item* would serve as abbreviations for 'iterum' or 'again'. Hilliard is making a clear distinction between white lead and the non-metallic ceruse which he used. There was much confusion in the naming of whites (see Harley, pp.154–6).

55. i.e. of ceruse. This section is the most frequently quoted part of the *Treatise* in seventeenth-century works on limning.

56. The missing word is supplied by *A Drawing Book.*

57. Hilliard may be thinking in particular of Levina Teerlinc; appointed 'paintrix' to Henry VIII around 1546, she held the same position under Edward VI, Mary and Elizabeth. She died in 1576; none of her work has been positively identified, but it seems very probable that as one of the leading limners of the generation between Holbein and Hilliard she influenced, and possibly even gave instruction to, the young Hilliard.

58. Sealed with clay, mixed in this case, with salt.

59. Be fired, as pots are fired.

60. The meaning is that other colours can be made by various mixtures of these five perfect colours; see also below, p.81.

61. The red colour used in the dyeing of a cloth of that name.

62. The soda or potash solution with which fat was saponified; see *Ure's Dictionary of Arts, Manufactures, and Mines* by Robert Hunt (7th edn. 1878), under 'Soap', and see Harley, p.59.

63. Reading from *A Drawing Book.* See also the anonymous *A Book of Drawing, Limning, Washing or Colouring of Maps and Prints and the Art of Painting etc.* (London, 1666), p.13, for the use of sap green for shadowing.

64. Allayed; see Alexander Browne, *Ars Pictoria* (1669), p.95; Browne

quotes the whole of the passage concerning pearls, under the heading 'Additional Observations out of a *Manuscript* of Mr. *Hilliards* touching *Miniture*'.

65. Browne's version adds here: 'But note your silver be laid round and full' (p.95). Many sixteenth and seventeenth-century miniatures suffer from the tarnishing of the silver, particularly noticeable in the pearls.

66. i.e. in the same colour; see Haydocke, *The Fourth Booke: of Light*, p.177: 'ever avoiding the shaddowes of contrary colours which some vse; by shaddowing Scarlet with blacke, yeallowe with sad tawny, blewe with sad ashcolour, and white also with a colour which hath no affinity with it for a shaddow; (as all colours saue blacke) which is onely his true shaddowe, being first lightned with white.' Dürer makes the same point in a MS in the British Library: 'Wherefore be careful that thou shade each colour with a similar colour. Thus I hold that a yellow, to retain its kind, must be shaded with a yellow, darker toned than the principal colour.' (Add. MS. 5231, translated in W. M. Conway, *The Writings of Albrecht Dürer* [1958], p.173). The notion that shadowing 'in his kind' is absurd is difficult, since it seems to be Hilliard's practice. Either there is a scribal error here, or Hilliard is simply pointing out that one cannot take this desirable practice to the extreme.

67. Topographical painting in water colours, as opposed to limning; Peacham advised learners to exercise 'your Pencill in washing and colouring small Tables of Countries and places, which at your leasure you may in one fortnight easily learne to doe' (*The Compleat Gentleman*, 1634, p.65).

68. Pope-Hennessy feels that Hilliard only 'conceives the five precious stones as the bodies towards whose properties the five colours used by the miniaturist aspire' (p.99); this aspect of Hilliard's analogy is certainly important, but so too is one that Pope-Hennessy denies: namely the use of naturally occurring stones to underline the natural, and thus divinely-sanctioned, status of the colours with which they correspond. The suggestion of a hierarchy of stones also underlines the idea of a hierarchy of colours, as of nature and society, in a typically Elizabethan manner. The analogy with the rainbow works in a similar way. Compare Peacham's *The Compleat Gentleman*, pp.154–9. Of Peacham's list of ways of blazoning, 'three onely are ancient, and of most use with us, viz. By Colours, By Planets, and By Precious stones'. Hilliard's choice of precious stones would be suitable to his argument, since Peacham argues that 'For the Nobility, your Blazon by precious stones is most correspondent' (p.160).

69. Originally meaning 'from the East', the word was eventually applied to any stone of very high quality.

70. See above, p.73 and note 60.

71. German.

72. Transparency and lustre.

73. See above, p.73 and note 53, for what seems to be a disagreement with Haydocke, to whom the 'you' in this rather vehement passage may refer.

74. So named from its place of origin near Samarcand; it is a variety of the spinel ruby, and not a true ruby.

75. A name for almandine, derived from the city of Syriam, in Burma, where such stones were cut and sold.

76. Hilliard's mention of this stone (a variety of garnet) antedates the earliest use recorded by *OED* by nearly 200 years.

77. The references may be to emeralds mined in the 'old world' as opposed to those which were beginning to arrive from the 'new mines' of South America during the sixteenth century; however, emeralds were mined in the Salzburg Alps from the Middle Ages, and Hilliard may think of these as the 'new mines' as opposed to the 'old mines' of much earlier times, such as those in Upper Egypt which were supposed to have supplied Cleopatra.

78. Though there is no independent text to confirm this emendation, it almost certainly restores the sense, if not the exact words, of the original.

79. Thomas Blount's *Glossographia* (1656) notes that 'Jewellers call that Tent which they put under Table Diamonds when they set them in work, and is made of mastick and turpentine'. The *OED* (under 'tent') quotes Sir Hugh Plat's *The Jewell house of art and nature* (1594) which mentions 'an excellent tent for a Diamond' made of ivory burnt in a crucible and the resulting powder mixed with oil of mastic.

80. The copyist was evidently unable to read a word here, and it may therefore be that Hilliard had some more recondite simile in mind.

81. One assumes this is akin to *verre eglomisé*, a delicate technique described by Cennino d'Andrea Cennini, *The Craftsman's Handbook*, translated by Daniel V. Thompson, Jr. (New York, 1960), pp.112–4.

82. Finely ground horn, used for making black; see above, 'velvet black', p.71, and *Miniatura*, p.94 for the preparation of 'Harts horn or Ivory Black'. Waste cuttings and raspings were often obtained from comb makers, and old bone utensils were also used.

83. The action of placing in position.

84. The reading is from MS.Harl.6000.

85. The distinction made between 'strokes' and 'pricks' reflects the characteristic techniques of Hilliard and Oliver respectively. See Hill-

iard's description of hatching for shadowing, p.81 above. The insertion of *rather* is supported by the version of this passage in *Miniatura.*

A SELECT BOOK LIST

The place of publication is London unless otherwise stated.

Erna Auerbach, *Nicholas Hilliard* (1961).

Erna Auerbach, *Tudor Artists: A Study of Painters in the Royal Service and of Portraiture on Illuminated Documents from the Accession of Henry VIII to the Death of Elizabeth I* (1954).

John Bate, *The Mysteries of Nature and Art* (2nd ed., 1634).

Noel Blakiston, 'Nicholas Hilliard and Queen Elizabeth's Third Great Seal', *Burlington Magazine*, XC (1948), 101–7.

A Book of Drawing, Limning, Washing or Colouring of Maps and Prints and the Art of Painting (1666).

Alexander Browne, *Ars Pictoria: or an Academy treating of Drawing, Painting, Limning, and Etching* (1669 and 1675).

Alexander Browne, *The Whole Art of Drawing, Painting, Limning, and Etching* (1660).

J. Southerden Burn (ed.), *Livre des Anglois à Genève* (1831).

Cennino d'Andrea Cennini, *Il libro dell'arte*, translated D. V. Thompson, *The Craftsman's Handbook* (New Haven, 1933).

Anna Somers Cocks et al, *Princely Magnificence: Court Jewels of the Renaissance, 1500–1630* (1980).

T. H. Colding, *Aspects of Miniature Painting* (Copenhagen, 1953).

Raphaëlle Costa de Beauregard, *Nicholas Hilliard et l'imaginaire élisabéthain* (Paris, 1991).

Mary Edmond, *Hilliard and Oliver* (1983).

Joan Evans, *English Jewellery from the fifth century A.D. to 1800* (1921).

Joan Evans, *A History of Jewellery 1100–1870* (1970).

Daphne Foskett, *A Dictionary of British Miniature Painters*, 2 vols. (1972).

E. P. Goldschmidt, 'Nicholas Hilliard as Wood Engraver', *TLS*, 9th August, 1947, p.403.

Yvonne Hackenbroch, *Renaissance Jewellery* (1979).

R. D. Harley, *Artists' Pigments c.1600–1835* (1970).

Richard Haydocke, *A Tracte containing the Artes of curious Paintinge Caruinge & Buildinge* (Oxford, 1598).

Leslie Hotson, *Shakespeare by Hilliard* (1977).

Nicholas Hilliard's Art of Limning, ed. Arthur F. Kinney and Linda Bradley Salamon (Boston, 1983).

Giovanni Paolo Lomazzo, *Trattato dell'arte della pittura, scoltura ed architettura* (Milan, 1584).

Basil S. Long, *British Miniaturists 1520–1860* (1929).

R. B. McKerrow & F. S. Ferguson, *Title-page Borders Used in England and Scotland, 1485–1640* (1932).

John Murdoch, Jim Murrell, Patrick J. Noon and Roy Strong, *The English Miniature* (1981).

V. J. Murrell, 'Cooper's painting technique', in Daphne Foskett, *Samuel Cooper and his Contemporaries* (1974), pp.xix–xxi.

Edward Norgate, *Miniatura or the Art of Limning*, ed. Martin Hardie (Oxford, 1919).

Philip Norman (ed.), 'Nicholas Hilliard's Treatise Concerning "The Arte of Limning", with Introduction and Notes by Philip Norman, LL.D.', *Walpole Society*, I (1911–12), pp.1–54.

Francesco Pacheco, *Arte de la pintura* ed. F. J. Sanchez Canton, 2 vols, (Madrid, 1956).

Henry Peacham, *The Art of Drawing with the Pen, and Limming in Water Colours* (1606).

Henry Peacham, *The Compleat Gentleman* (Oxford, 1906, based on 2nd ed. of 1634).

Henry Peacham, *The Gentlemans Exercise* (1612).

Henry Peacham, *Graphice or the Most Auncient and Excellent Art of Drawing and Limming* (1612).

David Piper, 'The 1590 Lumley Inventory: Hilliard, Segar and the Earl of Essex', I & II *Burlington Magazine*, XCIX (1957) 224–231, and 299–303.

John Pope-Hennessy, *A Lecture on Nicholas Hilliard* (1949).

John Pope-Hennessy, 'Nicholas Hilliard and Mannerist Art Theory', *JWCI*, VI (1943), 89–100.

Princely Magnificence: Court Jewels of the Renaissance, 1500–1630 (V&A Exhibition Catalogue, 1980).

Graham Reynolds, *English Portrait Miniatures* (1952).

Graham Reynolds, *Nicholas Hilliard and Isaac Oliver* (2nd ed. 1971).

Graham Reynolds, 'Portraits by Nicholas Hilliard and his Assistants of

King James I and his Family', *Walpole Society*, XXXIV (1952–54), 14–26.

William Salmon, *Polygraphice; or the Art of Drawing, Engraving, Etching, Limning, Painting, Washing, Varnishing, Colouring and Dying* (1672).

William Sanderson, *Graphice. The use of Pen and Pensil. Or, the most excellent Art of Painting* (1658).

Lindsay Stainton and Christopher White, *Drawing in England from Hilliard to Hogarth* (1987).

Roy Strong, *Artists of the Tudor Court* (1983).

Roy Strong, *The Cult of Elizabeth: Elizabethan Portraiture and Pageantry* (1977).

Roy Strong, *The English Icon: Elizabethan and Jacobean Portraiture* (1969).

Roy Strong, *National Portrait Gallery: Tudor and Jacobean Portraits*, 2 vols. (1969).

Roy Strong, *The English Renaissance Miniature* (revised edn. 1984).

Roy Strong, *Nicholas Hilliard* (1975).

Roy Strong, 'Queen Elizabeth, the Earl of Essex and Hilliard', *Burlington Magazine*, CI (1959), 145–9.

Theophilus, *De Diuersis Artibus*, translated C. R. Dodwell (1961).

D. V. Thompson, *The Materials of Medieval Painting* (1936).

A very proper treatise, wherein is briefly sett forthe the arte of Limming (1573).

Frances B. Troup, 'Biography of John Bodley, Father of Sir Thomas Bodley', *Transactions of the Devonshire Association*, XXXV (1903), 167–197.

Horace Walpole, Earl of Orford, *Anecdotes of Painting in England*, edited with additions by the Rev. J. Dallaway, 5 vols. (1826–28).

Carl Winter, *The British School of Miniature Portrait Painters* (1949).

Carl Winter, 'Hilliard and Elizabethan Miniatures', *Burlington Magazine*, LXXXIX (1947), 175–183.

Carl Winter, *Elizabethan Miniatures* (1943).